Essays on Education

By

HERBERT SPENCER

INTRODUCTION

The four essays on education which Herbert Spencer published in a single volume in 1861 were all written and separately published between 1854 and 1859. Their tone was aggressive and their proposals revolutionary; although all the doctrines—with one important exception—had already been vigorously preached by earlier writers on education, as Spencer himself was at pains to point out. The doctrine which was comparatively new ran through all four essays; but was most amply stated in the essay first published in 1859 under the title "What Knowledge is of Most Worth?" In this essay Spencer divided the leading kinds of human activity into those which minister to self-preservation, those which secure the necessaries of life, those whose end is the care of offspring, those which make good citizens, and those which prepare adults to enjoy nature, literature, and the fine arts; and he then maintained that in each of these several classes, knowledge of science was worth more than any other knowledge. He argued that everywhere throughout creation faculties are developed through the performance of the appropriate functions; so that it would be contrary to the whole harmony of nature "if one kind of culture were needed for the gaining of information, and another kind were needed as a mental gymnastic." He then maintained that the sciences are superior in all respects to languages as educational material; they train the memory better, and a superior kind of memory; they cultivate the judgment, and they impart an admirable moral and religious discipline. He concluded that "for discipline, as well as for guidance, science is of chiefest value. In all its effects, learning the meaning of things is better than learning the meaning of words." He answered the question "what knowledge is of most worth?" with the one word—science.

This doctrine was extremely repulsive to the established profession of education in England, where Latin, Greek, and mathematics had been the staples of education for many generations, and were believed to afford the only suitable preparation for the learned professions, public life, and cultivated society. In proclaiming this doctrine with ample illustration, ingenious argument, and forcible reiteration, Spencer was a true educational pioneer, although some of his scientific contemporaries were really preaching similar doctrines, each in his own field.

The profession of teaching has long been characterised by certain habitual convictions, which Spencer undertook to shake rudely, and even to deride. The first of these convictions is that all education, physical, intellectual, and moral, must be authoritative, and need take no account of the natural wishes, tendencies, and motives of the ignorant and undeveloped child. The second dominating conviction is that to teach means to tell, or show, children what they ought to see, believe, and utter. Expositions by the teacher and books are therefore the true means of education. The third and supreme conviction is that the method of education which produced the teacher himself and the contemporary or earlier scholars, authors, and publicists, must be the righteous and sufficient method. Its fruits demonstrate its soundness, and make it sacred. Herbert Spencer, in the essays included in the present volume, assaulted all three of these firm convictions. Accordingly, the ideas on education which he put forth more than fifty years ago have penetrated educational practice very slowly—particularly in England; but they are now coming to prevail in most civilised countries, and they will prevail more and more. Through him, the thoughts on education of Comenius, Montaigne, Locke, Milton, Rousseau, Pestalozzi, and other noted writers on this neglected subject are at last winning their way into practice, with the modifications or adaptations which the immense gains of the human race in knowledge and power since the nineteenth century opened have shown to be wise.

For teachers and educational administrators it is interesting to observe the steps by which Spencer's doctrines—and especially his doctrine of the supreme value of science—have advanced towards acceptance in practice. In general, the advance has been brought about through the indirect effects of the enormous industrial, social, and political changes of the last fifty years. The first practical step was the introduction of laboratory teaching of one or more of the sciences into the secondary schools and colleges. Chemistry and physics were the commonest subjects selected. These two subjects had been taught from books even earlier; but memorising science out of books is far less useful as training than memorising grammars and vocabularies. The characteristic discipline of science can be imparted only through the laboratory method. The schoolmasters and college faculties who took this step by no means admitted Spencer's contention that science should be the universal staple at all stages of child development. On the contrary, they believed, as most people do to-day, that the mind of the young child cannot grasp the processes and generalisations of science, and that science is no more universally fitted to develop mental power than the classics or mathematics. Indeed, experience during the past fifty years seems to have proved that fewer minds are naturally inclined to scientific study than to linguistic or historical study; so that if some science is to be learnt by everybody, the amount of such study should be limited to acquiring in one or two sciences knowledge of the scientific method in general. So much scientific training is indeed universally desirable; because good training of the senses to observe accurately is universally desirable, and the collecting, comparing, and grouping of many facts teach orderliness in thinking, and lead up to something which Spencer valued highly in education—"a rational explanation of phenomena."

Science having obtained a foothold in secondary schools and colleges, an adequate development of science-teaching resulted from the introduction of options or elections for the pupils among numerous different courses, in place of a curriculum prescribed for all. The elaborate teaching of many sciences was thus introduced. The pupil or student saw and recorded for himself; used books only as helps and guides in seeing, recording, and generalising; proceeded from the known to the unknown; and in short, made numerous applications of the doctrines which pervade all Spencer's writings on education. In the United States these methods were introduced earlier and have been carried farther than in England; but within the last few years the changes made in education have been more extensive and rapid in England than in any other country;—witness the announcements of the new high schools and the re-organised grammar schools, of such colleges as South Kensington, Armstrong, King's, the University College London, and Goldsmiths', and of the new municipal universities such as Victoria, Bristol, Sheffield, Birmingham, Liverpool, and Leeds. The new technical schools also illustrate the advent of instruction in applied science as an important element in advanced education. Such institutions as the Seafield Park Engineering College, the City Guilds of London Institute, the City of London College, and the Battersea Polytechnic are instances of the same development. Some endowed institutions for girls illustrate the same tendencies, as, for example, the Bedford College for Women and the Royal Holloway College. All these institutions teach sciences in considerable variety, and in the way that Spencer advocated,—not so much because they have distinctly accepted his views, as because modern industrial and social conditions compel the preparation in science of young people destined for various occupations and services indispensable to modern society. The method of the preparation is essentially that which he advocated.

Spencer's propositions to the effect that the study of science was desirable for artisans, artists, and, in general, for people who were to get their livings through various skills of hand and eye, were received with great incredulity, not to say derision—particularly when he maintained that some knowledge of the theory which underlies an art was desirable for manual practitioners of the art; but the changes of the last fifty years in the practice of the arts and trades may be said to have demonstrated that his views were thoroughly sound. The applications of science in the arts and trades have been so numerous and productive, that widespread training in science has become indispensable to any nation which means to excel in the manufacturing industries, whether of large scale or small scale. The extraordinary popularity of evening schools and correspondence schools in the United States rests on the need which young people employed in the various industries of the country feel of obtaining more theoretical knowledge about the physical or chemical processes through which they are earning a livelihood. The Young Men's Christian Associations in the American cities have become great centres of evening instruction for just such young persons. The correspondence schools are teaching hundreds of thousands of young people at work in machine-shops, mills, mines, and factories, who believe that they can advance themselves in their several occupations by supplementing their elementary education with correspondence courses, taken while they are at work earning a livelihood in industries that rest ultimately on applications of science.

Spencer's objection to the constant exercise of authority and compulsion in schools, families, and the State is felt to-day much more widely than it was in 1858, when he wrote his essay on moral education. His proposal that children should be allowed to suffer the natural consequences of their foolish or wrong acts does not seem to the present generation—any more than it did to him—to be applicable to very young children, who need protection from the undue severity of many natural penalties; but the soundness of his general doctrine that it is the true function of parents and teachers to see that children habitually experience the normal consequences of their conduct, without putting artificial consequences in place of them, now commands the assent of most persons whose minds have been freed from the theological dogmas of original sin and total depravity. Spencer did not expect the immediate adoption of this principle; because society as a whole was not yet humane enough. He admitted that the uncontrollable child of ill-controlled adults might sometimes have to be scolded or beaten, and that these barbarous methods might be "perhaps the best preparation such children can have for the barbarous society in which they are presently to play a part." He hoped, however, that the civilised members of society would by and by spontaneously use milder measures; and this hope has been realised in good degree, with the result that happiness in childhood is much commoner and more constant than it used to be. Parents and teachers are beginning to realise that self-control is a prime object in moral education, and that this self-control cannot be practised under a regime of constant supervision, unexplained commands, and painful punishments, but must be gained in freedom. Some large-scale experience with American secondary schools which prepare boys for admission to college has been edifying in this respect. The American colleges, as a rule, do not undertake to exercise much supervision over their students, but leave them free to regulate their own lives in regard to both work and play. Now it is the boys who come from the secondary schools where the closest supervision is maintained that are in most danger of falling into evil ways when they first go to college.

Spencer put very forcibly a valuable doctrine for which many earlier writers on the theory of education had failed to get a hearing—the doctrine, namely, that all instruction should be pleasurable and interesting. Fifty years ago almost all teachers believed that it was impossible to make school-work interesting, or life-work either; so that the child must be forced to grind without pleasure, in preparation for life's grind; and the forcing was to be done by experience of the teacher's displeasure and the infliction of pain. Through the slow effects of Spencer's teaching and of the experience of practical teachers who have demonstrated that instruction can be made pleasurable, and that the very hardest work is done by interested pupils because they are interested, it has gradually come to pass that his heresy has become the prevailing judgment among sensible and humane teachers. The experience of many adults, hard at work in the modern industrial, commercial, and financial world, has taught them that human beings can make their intensest application only to problems in which they are personally interested for one reason or another, and that freemen work much harder than slaves, because they feel within themselves strong motives for exertion which slaves cannot possibly feel. So, many intelligent adults, including many parents and teachers, have come to believe it possible that children will learn to do hard work, both in school and in after life, through the free play of interior motives which appeal to them, and prompt them to persistent exertion.

The justice of Spencer's views about training through pleasurable sensation and achievement in freedom rather than through uninterested work and pain inflicted by despotic government, is well illustrated by the recent improvements in the discipline of reformatories for boys and girls and young men and women. It has been demonstrated that the only useful reformatories are those which diminish the criminal's liberty of action as little as possible, require him to perform productive labour, educate him for a trade or other useful occupation, and offer him the reward of an abridgment of sentence in return for industry and self-control. Repression and compulsion under penalties however severe fail to reform, and often make bad moral conditions worse. Instruction, as much freedom as is consistent with the safety of society, and an appeal to the ordinary motives of emulation, satisfaction in achievement, and the desire to win credit, can, and do, reform.

Many schools, both public and private, have now adopted—in most cases unconsciously—many of Spencer's more detailed suggestions. The laboratory method of instruction, for example, now common for scientific subjects in good schools, is an application of his doctrines of concrete illustration, training in the accurate use of the senses, and subordination of book-work. Many schools realise, too, that learning by heart and, in general, memorising from books are not the only means of storing the mind of a child. They should make parts of a sound education, but should not be used to the exclusion of learning through eye, ear, and hand. Spencer pointed out with much elaboration that children acquire in their early years a vast amount of information exclusively through the incessant use of their senses. To-day teachers know this fact, and realise much better than the teachers of fifty years ago did, that all through the school and college period the pupils should be getting a large part of their new knowledge through the careful application of their own powers of observation, aided, indeed, by books and pictures which record the observations, old and new, of other people. The young human being, unlike the puppy or the kitten, is not confined to the use of his own senses as sources of information and discovery; but can enjoy the fruits of a prodigious width and depth of observation acquired by preceding generations and adult members of his own generation. A recent illustration of this extension of the method of observation in teaching to observations made by other people is the new method of giving moral instruction to school children through photographs of actual scenes which illustrate both good morals and bad, the exhibition of the photographs being accompanied by a running oral comment from the teacher. In this kind of moral instruction it seems to be possible to interest all kinds of children, both civilised and barbarous, both ill-bred and well-bred. The teaching comes through the eye, for the children themselves observe intently the pictures which the lantern throws on the screen; but the striking scenes thus put before them probably lie in most instances quite outside the region of their own experiences.

The essay on "What Knowledge is of Most Worth?" contains a hot denunciation of that kind of information which in most schools used to usurp the name of history. It is enough to say of this part of Spencer's educational doctrine that all the best historical writers since the middle of the nineteenth century seem to have adopted the principles which he declared should govern the writing of history. As a result, the teaching of history in schools and colleges has undergone a profound change. It now deals with the nature and action of government, central, local, and ecclesiastical, with social observances, industrial systems, and the customs which regulate popular life, out-of-doors and indoors. It depicts also the intellectual condition of the nation and the progress it has made in applied science, the fine arts, and legislation, and includes descriptions of the peoples' food, shelters, and amusements. To this result many authors and teachers have contributed; but Spencer's violent denunciation of history as it was taught in his time has greatly promoted this important reform.

Many twentieth-century teachers are sure to put in practice Spencer's exhortation to teach children to draw with pen and pencil, and to use paints and brush. He maintained that the common omission of drawing as an important element in the training of children was in contempt of some of the most obvious of nature's suggestions with regard to the natural development of human faculties; and the better recent practice in some English and American schools verifies his statement; nevertheless some of the best secondary schools in both countries still fail to recognise drawing and painting as important elements in liberal education.

Modern society as yet hardly approaches the putting into effective practice of the sound views which Spencer set forth with great detail in his essay on "Physical Education." The instruction given in schools and colleges on the care of the body and the laws of health is still very meagre; and in certain subjects of the utmost importance no instruction whatever is given, as, for example, in the normal methods of reproduction in plants and animals, in eugenics, and in the ruinous consequences of disregarding sexual purity and honour. In one respect his fundamental doctrine of freedom, carried into the domain of physical exercise, has been extensively adopted in England, on the Continent, and in America. He taught that although gymnastics, military drill, and formal exercises of the limbs are better than nothing, they can never serve in place of the plays prompted by nature. He maintained that "for girls as well as boys the sportive activities to which the instincts impel are essential to bodily welfare." This principle is now being carried into practice not only for school-children, but for operatives in factories, clerks, and other young persons whose occupations are sedentary and monotonous. For all such persons, free plays are vastly better than formal exercises of any sort.

The wide adoption of Spencer's educational ideas has had to await the advent of the new educational administration and the new public interest therein. It awaited the coming of the state university in the United States and of the city university in England, the establishment of numerous technical schools, the profound modifications made in grammar schools and academies, and the multiplication in both countries of the secondary schools called high schools. In other words, his ideas gradually gained admission to a vast number of new institutions of education, which were created and maintained because both the governments and the nations felt a new sense of responsibility for the training of the future generations. These new agencies have been created in great variety, and the introduction of Spencer's ideas has been much facilitated by this variety. These institutions were national, state, or municipal. They were tax-supported or endowed. They charged tuition fees, or were open to competent children or adults without fee. They undertook to meet alike the needs of the individual and the needs of the community; and this undertaking involved the introduction of many new subjects of instruction and many new methods. Through their variety they could be sympathetic with both individualism and collectivism. The variety of instruction offered is best illustrated in the strongest American universities, some of which are tax-supported and some endowed. These universities maintain a great variety of courses of instruction in subjects none of which was taught with the faintest approach to adequacy in American universities sixty years ago; but in making these extensions the universities have not found it necessary to reduce the instruction offered in the classics and mathematics. The traditional cultural studies are still provided; but they represent only one programme among many, and no one is compelled to follow it. The domination of the classics is at an end; but any student who prefers the traditional path to culture, or whose parents choose that path for him, will find in several American universities much richer provisions of classical instruction than any university in the country offered sixty years ago. The present proposals to widen the influence of Oxford University do not mean, therefore, that the classics, history, and philosophy are to be taught less there, but only that other subjects are to be taught more, and that a greater number and variety of young men will be prepared there for the service of the nation.

The new public interest in education as a necessary of modern industrial and political life has gradually brought about a great increase in the proportional number of young men and women whose education is prolonged beyond the period of primary or elementary instruction; and this multitude of young people is preparing for a great variety of callings, many of which are new within sixty years, having been brought into being by the extraordinary advances of applied science. The advent of these new callings has favoured the spread of Spencer's educational ideas. The recent agitation in favour of what is called vocational training is a vivid illustration of the wide acceptance of his arguments. Even the farmers, their farm-hands, and their children must nowadays be offered free instruction in agriculture; because the public, and especially the urban public, believes that by disseminating better methods of tillage, better seed, and appropriate manures, the yield of the farms can be improved in quality and multiplied in quantity. In regard to all material interests, the free peoples are acting on the principle that science is the knowledge of most worth. Spencer's doctrine of natural consequences in place of artificial penalties, his view that all young people should be taught how to be wise parents and good citizens, and his advocacy of instruction in public and private hygiene, lie at the roots of many of the philanthropic and reformatory movements of the day.

On the whole, Herbert Spencer has been fortunate among educational philosophers. He has not had to wait so long for the acceptance of his teachings as Comenius, Montaigne, or Rousseau waited. His ideas have been floated on a prodigious tide of industrial and social change, which necessarily involved wide-spread and profound educational reform.

This introduction deals with Spencer's four essays on education; but in the present volume are included three other famous essays written by him during the same period 1854-59 which produced the essays on education. All three are germane to the educational essays, because they deal with the general law of human progress, with the genesis of that science which Spencer thought to be the knowledge of most worth, and with the origin and function of music, a subject which he maintained should play an important part in any scheme of education.

CHARLES W. ELIOT.

SELECT BIBLIOGRAPHY

WORKS. *The Proper Sphere of Government*, 1843; *Social Statics*, 1850; *Theory of Population Westminster Review*, April 1852; *The Development of Hypothesis The Leader*, 20th March 1852; *The Ultimate Laws of Physiology National Review*, April 1857; *Essays, Scientific, Political and Speculative*, 2 vols., 1858-63; *Education*, 1861; *A System of Synthetic Philosophy* 12 vols., 1862-96, made up as follows: *First Principles*, 1862; *Principles of Biology*, 2 vols., 1864-7; *Principles of Psychology*, 2 vols., 1870-2; *Principles of Sociology*, 3 vols., 1876-96; *Ceremonial Institutions*, 1879; *Principles of Morality*, 2 vols., 1879-93 vol. i, part I published as *Data of Ethics*, 1879; part 4 as *Justice*, 1891; *Political Institutions*, 1882. Meanwhile the following works were also published: *The Classification of the Sciences*, 1864; *The Study of Sociology*, 1872; *Descriptive Sociology*, 1873; *The Man versus the State*, 1884; *The Factors of Organic Evolution*, 1887; *The Inadequacy of Natural Selection*, 1893. Spencer's *Autobiography* appeared posthumously, 2 vols., 1904.

COLLECTED EDITION. Nineteen volumes, 1861-1902.

BIOGRAPHY AND CRITICISM. T. Funk-Brentano, *Les Sophistes grecs et les Sophistes contemporains* Mill and Spencer, 1879; F.H. Collins, *An Epitome of the Synthetic Philosophy*, 1889; H. Sidgwick, *Lectures on the Ethics of Green, Spencer and Martineau*, 1902; 'The Philosophy of Herbert Spencer' in *The Philosophy of Kant and Other Lectures*, 1905; D. Duncan, *An Introduction to the Philosophy of Spencer*, 1904; *Life and Letters of Herbert Spencer*, 1908; J. Royce, *Herbert Spencer. An Estimate and a Review*, 1904; J.A. Thomson, *Herbert Spencer*, 1906; W.H. Hudson, *Herbert Spencer*, 1916; J. Rumney, *Herbert Spencer's Sociology*, 1934; R.C.K. Ensor, *Some Reflections on Herbert Spencer's Doctrine*, 1946.

CONTENTS

PAGE

Introduction by Charles W. Eliot   vii

PART I

EDUCATION: INTELLECTUAL, MORAL, AND PHYSICAL

WHAT KNOWLEDGE IS OF MOST WORTH?	1
INTELLECTUAL EDUCATION	45
MORAL EDUCATION	84
PHYSICAL EDUCATION	116

PART II

ESSAYS ON KINDRED SUBJECTS

PROGRESS: ITS LAW AND CAUSE	153
ON MANNERS AND FASHION	198
ON THE GENESIS OF SCIENCE	239
ON THE PHYSIOLOGY OF LAUGHTER	298
ON THE ORIGIN AND FUNCTION OF MUSIC	310

ORIGINAL PREFACE

TO

EDUCATION: INTELLECTUAL, MORAL, AND PHYSICAL

The four chapters of which this work consists, originally appeared as four Review-articles: the first in the *Westminster Review* for July 1859; the second in the *North British Review* for May 1854; and the remaining two in the *British Quarterly Review* for April 1858 and for April 1859. Severally treating different divisions of the subject, but together forming a tolerably complete whole, I originally wrote them with a view to their republication in a united form; and they would some time since have thus been issued, had not a legal difficulty stood in the way. This difficulty being now removed, I hasten to fulfil the intention with which they were written.

That in their first shape these chapters were severally independent, is the reason to be assigned for some slight repetitions which occur in them: one leading idea, more especially, reappearing twice. As, however, this idea is on each occasion presented under a new form, and as it can scarcely be too much enforced, I have not thought well to omit any of the passages embodying it.

Some additions of importance will be found in the chapter on Intellectual Education; and in the one on Physical Education there are a few minor alterations. But the chief changes which have been made, are changes of expression: all of the essays having undergone a careful verbal revision.

H.S.

London, *May 1861*

SPENCER'S ESSAYS

PART I—ON EDUCATION

WHAT KNOWLEDGE IS OF MOST WORTH?

It has been truly remarked that, in order of time, decoration precedes dress. Among people who submit to great physical suffering that they may have themselves handsomely tattooed, extremes of temperature are borne with but little attempt at mitigation. Humboldt tells us that an Orinoco Indian, though quite regardless of bodily comfort, will yet labour for a fortnight to purchase pigment wherewith to make himself admired; and that the same woman who would not hesitate to leave her hut without a fragment of clothing on, would not dare to commit such a breach of decorum as to go out unpainted. Voyagers find that coloured beads and trinkets are much more prized by wild tribes than are calicoes or broadcloths. And the anecdotes we have of the ways in which, when shirts and coats are given, savages turn them to some ludicrous display, show how completely the idea of ornament predominates over that of use. Nay, there are still more extreme illustrations: witness the fact narrated by Capt. Speke of his African attendants, who strutted about in their goat-skin mantles when the weather was fine, but when it was wet, took them off, folded them up, and went about naked, shivering in the rain! Indeed, the facts of aboriginal life seem to indicate that dress is developed out of decorations. And when we remember that even among ourselves most think more about the fineness of the fabric than its warmth, and more about the cut than the convenience—when we see that the function is still in great measure subordinated to the appearance—we have further reason for inferring such an origin.

It is curious that the like relations hold with the mind. Among mental as among bodily acquisitions, the ornamental comes before the useful. Not only in times past, but almost as much in our own era, that knowledge which conduces to personal well-being has been postponed to that which brings applause. In the Greek schools, music, poetry, rhetoric, and a philosophy which, until Socrates taught, had but little bearing upon action, were the dominant subjects; while knowledge aiding the arts of life had a very subordinate place. And in our own universities and schools at the present moment, the like antithesis holds. We are guilty of something like a platitude when we say that throughout his after-career, a boy, in nine cases out of ten, applies his Latin and Greek to no practical purposes. The remark is trite that in his shop, or his office, in managing his estate or his family, in playing his part as director of a bank or a railway, he is very little aided by this knowledge he took so many years to acquire—so little, that generally the greater part of it drops out of his memory; and if he occasionally vents a Latin quotation, or alludes to some Greek myth, it is less to throw light on the topic in hand than for the sake of effect. If we inquire what is the real motive for giving boys a classical education, we find it to be simply conformity to public opinion. Men dress their children's minds as they do their bodies, in the prevailing fashion. As the Orinoco Indian puts on paint before leaving his hut, not with a view to any direct benefit, but because he would be ashamed to be seen without it; so, a boy's drilling in Latin and Greek is insisted on, not because of their intrinsic value, but that he may not be disgraced by being found ignorant of them—that he may have "the education of a gentleman"—the badge marking a certain social position, and bringing a consequent respect.

This parallel is still more clearly displayed in the case of the other sex. In the treatment of both mind and body, the decorative element has continued to predominate in a greater degree among women than among men. Originally, personal adornment occupied the attention of both sexes equally. In these latter days of civilisation, however, we see that in the dress of men the regard for appearance has in a considerable degree yielded to the regard for comfort; while in their education the useful has of late been trenching on the ornamental. In neither direction has this change gone so far with women. The wearing of earrings, finger-rings, bracelets; the elaborate dressings of the hair; the still occasional use of paint; the immense labour bestowed in making habiliments sufficiently attractive; and the great discomfort that will be submitted to for the sake of conformity; show how greatly, in the attiring of women, the desire of approbation overrides the desire for warmth and convenience. And similarly in their education, the immense preponderance of "accomplishments" proves how here, too, use is subordinated to display. Dancing, deportment, the piano, singing, drawing—what a large space do these occupy! If you ask why Italian and German are learnt, you will find that, under all the sham reasons given, the real reason is, that a knowledge of those tongues is thought ladylike. It is not that the books written in them may be utilised, which they scarcely ever are; but that Italian and German songs may be sung, and that the extent of attainment may bring whispered admiration. The births, deaths, and marriages of kings, and other like historic trivialities, are committed to memory, not because of any direct benefits that can possibly result from knowing them: but because society considers them parts of a good education—because the absence of such knowledge may bring the contempt of others. When we have named reading, writing, spelling, grammar, arithmetic, and sewing, we have named about all the things a girl is taught with a view to their actual uses in life; and even some of these have more reference to the good opinion of others than to immediate personal welfare.

Thoroughly to realise the truth that with the mind as with the body the ornamental precedes the useful, it is requisite to glance at its rationale. This lies in the fact that, from the far past down even to the present, social needs have subordinated individual needs, and that the chief social need has been the control of individuals. It is not, as we commonly suppose, that there are no governments but those of monarchs, and parliaments, and constituted authorities. These acknowledged governments are supplemented by other unacknowledged ones, that grow up in all circles, in which every man or woman strives to be king or queen or lesser dignitary. To get above some and be reverenced by them, and to propitiate those who are above us, is the universal struggle in which the chief energies of life are expended. By the accumulation of wealth, by style of living, by beauty of dress, by display of knowledge or intellect, each tries to subjugate others; and so aids in weaving that ramified network of restraints by which society is kept in order. It is not the savage chief only, who, in formidable war-paint, with scalps at his belt, aims to strike awe into his inferiors; it is not only the belle who, by elaborate toilet, polished manners, and numerous accomplishments, strives to "make conquests;" but the scholar, the historian, the philosopher, use their acquirements to the same end. We are none of us content with quietly unfolding our own individualities to the full in all directions; but have a restless craving to impress our individualities upon others, and in some way subordinate them. And this it is which determines the character of our education. Not what knowledge is of most real worth, is the consideration; but what will bring most applause, honour, respect—what will most conduce to social position and influence—what will be most imposing. As, throughout life, not what we are, but what we shall be thought, is the question; so in education, the question is, not the intrinsic value of knowledge, so much as its extrinsic effects on others. And this being our dominant idea, direct utility is scarcely more regarded than by the barbarian when filing his teeth and staining his nails.

If there requires further evidence of the rude, undeveloped character of our education, we have it in the fact that the comparative worths of different kinds of knowledge have been as yet scarcely even discussed—much less discussed in a methodic way with definite results. Not only is it that no standard of relative values has yet been agreed upon; but the existence of any such standard has not been conceived in a clear manner. And not only is it that the existence of such a standard has not been clearly conceived; but the need for it seems to have been scarcely even felt. Men read books on this topic, and attend lectures on that; decide that their children shall be instructed in these branches of knowledge, and shall not be instructed in those; and all under the guidance of mere custom, or liking, or prejudice; without ever considering the enormous importance of determining in some rational way what things are really most worth learning. It is true that in all circles we hear occasional remarks on the importance of this or the other order of information. But whether the degree of its importance justifies the expenditure of the time needed to acquire it; and whether there are not things of more importance to which such time might be better devoted; are queries which, if raised at all, are disposed of quite summarily, according to personal predilections. It is true also, that now and then, we hear revived the standing controversy respecting the comparative merits of classics and mathematics. This controversy, however, is carried on in an empirical manner, with no reference to an ascertained criterion; and the question at issue is insignificant when compared with the general question of which it is part. To suppose that deciding whether a mathematical or a classical education is the best is deciding what is the proper *curriculum*, is much the same thing as to suppose that the whole of dietetics lies in ascertaining whether or not bread is more nutritive than potatoes!

The question which we contend is of such transcendent moment, is, not whether such or such knowledge is of worth but what is its *relative* worth? When they have named certain advantages which a given course of study has secured them, persons are apt to assume that they have justified themselves; quite forgetting that the adequateness of the advantages is the point to be judged. There is, perhaps, not a subject to which men devote attention that has not *some* value. A year diligently spent in getting up heraldry, would very possibly give a little further insight into ancient manners and morals. Any one who should learn the distances between all the towns in England, might, in the course of his life, find one or two of the thousand facts he had acquired of some slight service when arranging a journey. Gathering together all the small gossip of a county, profitless occupation as it would be, might yet occasionally help to establish some useful fact—say, a good example of hereditary transmission. But in these cases, every one would admit that there was no proportion between the required labour and the probable benefit. No one would tolerate the proposal to devote some years of a boy's time to getting such information, at the cost of much more valuable information which he might else have got. And if here the test of relative value is appealed to and held conclusive, then should it be appealed to and held conclusive throughout. Had we time to master all subjects we need not be particular. To quote the old song:—

Could a man be secure
That his day would endure
As of old, for a thousand long years,
What things might he know!

What deeds might he do!
And all without hurry or care.

"But we that have but span-long lives" must ever bear in mind our limited time for acquisition. And remembering how narrowly this time is limited, not only by the shortness of life, but also still more by the business of life, we ought to be especially solicitous to employ what time we have to the greatest advantage. Before devoting years to some subject which fashion or fancy suggests, it is surely wise to weigh with great care the worth of the results, as compared with the worth of various alternative results which the same years might bring if otherwise applied.

In education, then, this is the question of questions, which it is high time we discussed in some methodic way. The first in importance, though the last to be considered, is the problem—how to decide among the conflicting claims of various subjects on our attention. Before there can be a rational *curriculum*, we must settle which things it most concerns us to know; or, to use a word of Bacon's, now unfortunately obsolete—we must determine the relative values of knowledges.

To this end, a measure of value is the first requisite. And happily, respecting the true measure of value, as expressed in general terms, there can be no dispute. Every one in contending for the worth of any particular order of information, does so by showing its bearing upon some part of life. In reply to the question—"Of what use is it?" the mathematician, linguist, naturalist, or philosopher, explains the way in which his learning beneficially influences action—saves from evil or secures good—conduces to happiness. When the teacher of writing has pointed out how great an aid writing is to success in business—that is, to the obtainment of sustenance—that is, to satisfactory living; he is held to have proved his case. And when the collector of dead facts say a numismatist fails to make clear any appreciable effects which these facts can produce on human welfare, he is obliged to admit that they are comparatively valueless. All then, either directly or by implication, appeal to this as the ultimate test.

How to live?—that is the essential question for us. Not how to live in the mere material sense only, but in the widest sense. The general problem which comprehends every special problem is—the right ruling of conduct in all directions under all circumstances. In what way to treat the body; in what way to treat the mind; in what way to manage our affairs; in what way to bring up a family; in what way to behave as a citizen; in what way to utilise those sources of happiness which nature supplies—how to use all our faculties to the greatest advantage of ourselves and others—how to live completely? And this being the great thing needful for us to learn, is, by consequence, the great thing which education has to teach. To prepare us for complete living is the function which education has to discharge; and the only rational mode of judging of an educational course is, to judge in what degree it discharges such function.

This test, never used in its entirety, but rarely even partially used, and used then in a vague, half conscious way, has to be applied consciously, methodically, and throughout all cases. It behoves us to set before ourselves, and ever to keep clearly in view, complete living as the end to be achieved; so that in bringing up our children we may choose subjects and methods of instruction, with deliberate reference to this end. Not only ought we to cease from the mere unthinking adoption of the current fashion in education, which has no better warrant than any other fashion; but we must also rise above that rude, empirical style of judging displayed by those more intelligent people who do bestow some care in overseeing the cultivation of their children's minds. It must not suffice simply to *think* that such or such information will be useful in after life, or that this kind of knowledge is of more practical value than that; but we must seek out some process of estimating their respective values, so that as far as possible we may positively *know* which are most deserving of attention.

Doubtless the task is difficult—perhaps never to be more than approximately achieved. But, considering the vastness of the interests at stake, its difficulty is no reason for pusillanimously passing it by; but rather for devoting every energy to its mastery. And if we only proceed systematically, we may very soon get at results of no small moment.

Our first step must obviously be to classify, in the order of their importance, the leading kinds of activity which constitute human life. They may be naturally arranged into:—1. those activities which directly minister to self-preservation; 2. those activities which, by securing the necessaries of life, indirectly minister to self-preservation; 3. those activities which have for their end the rearing and discipline of offspring; 4. those activities which are involved in the maintenance of proper social and political relations; 5. those miscellaneous activities which fill up the leisure part of life, devoted to the gratification of the tastes and feelings.

That these stand in something like their true order of subordination, it needs no long consideration to show. The actions and precautions by which, from moment to moment, we secure personal safety, must clearly take precedence of all others. Could there be a man, ignorant as an infant of surrounding objects and movements, or how to guide himself among them, he would pretty certainly lose his life the first time he went into the street; notwithstanding any amount of learning he might have on other matters. And as entire ignorance in all other directions would be less promptly fatal than entire ignorance in this direction, it must be admitted that knowledge immediately conducive to self-preservation is of primary importance.

That next after direct self-preservation comes the indirect self-preservation which consists in acquiring the means of living, none will question. That a man's industrial functions must be considered before his parental ones, is manifest from the fact that, speaking generally, the discharge of the parental functions is made possible only by the previous discharge of the industrial ones. The power of self-maintenance necessarily preceding the power of maintaining offspring, it follows that knowledge needful for self-maintenance has stronger claims than knowledge needful for family welfare—is second in value to none save knowledge needful for immediate self-preservation.

As the family comes before the State in order of time—as the bringing up of children is possible before the State exists, or when it has ceased to be, whereas the State is rendered possible only by the bringing up of children; it follows that the duties of the parent demand closer attention than those of the citizen. Or, to use a further argument—since the goodness of a society ultimately depends on the nature of its citizens; and since the nature of its citizens is more modifiable by early training than by anything else; we must conclude that the welfare of the family underlies the welfare of society. And hence knowledge directly conducing to the first, must take precedence of knowledge directly conducing to the last.

Those various forms of pleasurable occupation which fill up the leisure left by graver occupations—the enjoyments of music, poetry, painting, etc.—manifestly imply a preexisting society. Not only is a considerable development of them impossible without a long-established social union; but their very subject-matter consists in great part of social sentiments and sympathies. Not only does society supply the conditions to their growth; but also the ideas and sentiments they express. And, consequently, that part of human conduct which constitutes good citizenship, is of more moment than that which goes out in accomplishments or exercise of the tastes; and, in education, preparation for the one must rank before preparation for the other.

Such then, we repeat, is something like the rational order of subordination:—That education which prepares for direct self-preservation; that which prepares for indirect self-preservation; that which prepares for parenthood; that which prepares for citizenship; that which prepares for the miscellaneous refinements of life. We do not mean to say that these divisions are definitely separable. We do not deny that they are intricately entangled with each other, in such way that there can be no training for any that is not in some measure a training for all. Nor do we question that of each division there are portions more important than certain portions of the preceding divisions: that, for instance, a man of much skill in business but little other faculty, may fall further below the standard of complete living than one of but moderate ability in money-getting but great judgment as a parent; or that exhaustive information bearing on right social action, joined with entire want of general culture in literature and the fine arts, is less desirable than a more moderate share of the one joined with some of the other. But, after making due qualifications, there still remain these broadly-marked divisions; and it still continues substantially true that these divisions subordinate one another in the foregoing order, because the corresponding divisions of life make one another *possible* in that order.

Of course the ideal of education is—complete preparation in all these divisions. But failing this ideal, as in our phase of civilisation every one must do more or less, the aim should be to maintain *a due proportion* between the degrees of preparation in each. Not exhaustive cultivation in any one, supremely important though it may be—not even an exclusive attention to the two, three, or four divisions of greatest importance; but an attention to all:—greatest where the value is greatest; less where the value is less; least where the value is least. For the average man not to forget the cases in which peculiar aptitude for some one department of knowledge, rightly makes pursuit of that one the bread-winning occupation—for the average man, we say, the desideratum is, a training that approaches nearest to perfection in the things which most subserve complete living, and falls more and more below perfection in the things that have more and more remote bearings on complete living.

In regulating education by this standard, there are some general considerations that should be ever present to us. The worth of any kind of culture, as aiding complete living, may be either necessary or more or less contingent. There is knowledge of intrinsic value; knowledge of quasi-intrinsic value; and knowledge of conventional value. Such facts as that sensations of numbness and tingling commonly precede paralysis, that the resistance of water to a body moving through it varies as the square of the velocity, that chlorine is a disinfectant,—these, and the truths of Science in general, are of intrinsic value: they will bear on human conduct ten thousand years hence as they do now. The extra knowledge of our own language, which is given by an acquaintance with Latin and Greek, may be considered to have a value that is quasi-intrinsic: it must exist for us and for other races whose languages owe much to these sources; but will last only as long as our languages last. While that kind of information which, in our schools, usurps the name History—the mere tissue of names and dates and dead unmeaning events—has a conventional value only: it has not the remotest bearing on any of our actions; and is of use only for the avoidance of those unpleasant criticisms which current opinion passes upon its absence. Of course, as those facts which concern all mankind throughout all time must be held of greater moment than those which concern only a portion of them during a limited era, and of far greater moment than those which concern only a portion of them during the continuance of a fashion; it follows that in a rational estimate, knowledge of intrinsic worth must, other things equal, take precedence of knowledge that is of quasi-intrinsic or conventional worth.

One further preliminary. Acquirement of every kind has two values—value as *knowledge* and value as *discipline*. Besides its use for guiding conduct, the acquisition of each order of facts has also its use as mental exercise; and its effects as a preparative for complete living have to be considered under both these heads.

These, then, are the general ideas with which we must set out in discussing a *curriculum*:— Life as divided into several kinds of activity of successively decreasing importance; the worth of each order of facts as regulating these several kinds of activity, intrinsically, quasi-intrinsically, and conventionally; and their regulative influences estimated both as knowledge and discipline.

Happily, that all-important part of education which goes to secure direct self-preservation, is in great part already provided for. Too momentous to be left to our blundering, Nature takes it into her own hands. While yet in its nurse's arms, the infant, by hiding its face and crying at the sight of a stranger, shows the dawning instinct to attain safety by flying from that which is unknown and may be dangerous; and when it can walk, the terror it manifests if an unfamiliar dog comes near, or the screams with which it runs to its mother after any startling sight or sound, shows this instinct further developed. Moreover, knowledge subserving direct self-preservation is that which it is chiefly busied in acquiring from hour to hour. How to balance its body; how to control its movements so as to avoid collisions; what objects are hard, and will hurt if struck; what objects are heavy, and injure if they fall on the limbs; which things will bear the weight of the body, and which not; the pains inflicted by fire, by missiles, by sharp instruments—these, and various other pieces of information needful for the avoidance of death or accident, it is ever learning. And when, a few years later, the energies go out in running, climbing, and jumping, in games of strength and games of skill, we see in all these actions by which the muscles are developed, the perceptions sharpened, and the judgment quickened, a preparation for the safe conduct of the body among surrounding objects and movements; and for meeting those greater dangers that occasionally occur in the lives of all. Being thus, as we say, so well cared for by Nature, this fundamental education needs comparatively little care from us. What we are chiefly called upon to see, is, that there shall be free scope for gaining this experience and receiving this discipline—that there shall be no such thwarting of Nature as that by which stupid schoolmistresses commonly prevent the girls in their charge from the spontaneous physical activities they would indulge in; and so render them comparatively incapable of taking care of themselves in circumstances of peril.

This, however, is by no means all that is comprehended in the education that prepares for direct self-preservation. Besides guarding the body against mechanical damage or destruction, it has to be guarded against injury from other causes—against the disease and death that follow breaches of physiologic law. For complete living it is necessary, not only that sudden annihilations of life shall be warded off; but also that there shall be escaped the incapacities and the slow annihilation which unwise habits entail. As, without health and energy, the industrial, the parental, the social, and all other activities become more or less impossible; it is clear that this secondary kind of direct self-preservation is only less important than the primary kind; and that knowledge tending to secure it should rank very high.

It is true that here, too, guidance is in some measure ready supplied. By our various physical sensations and desires, Nature has insured a tolerable conformity to the chief requirements. Fortunately for us, want of food, great heat, extreme cold, produce promptings too peremptory to be disregarded. And would men habitually obey these and all like promptings when less strong, comparatively few evils would arise. If fatigue of body or brain were in every case followed by desistance; if the oppression produced by a close atmosphere always led to ventilation; if there were no eating without hunger, or drinking without thirst; then would the system be but seldom out of working order. But so profound an ignorance is there of the laws of life, that men do not even know that their sensations are their natural guides, and when not rendered morbid by long—continued disobedience their trustworthy guides. So that though, to speak teleologically, Nature has provided efficient safeguards to health, lack of knowledge makes them in a great measure useless.

If any one doubts the importance of an acquaintance with the principles of physiology, as a means to complete living, let him look around and see how many men and women he can find in middle or later life who are thoroughly well. Only occasionally do we meet with an example of vigorous health continued to old age; hourly do we meet with examples of acute disorder, chronic ailment, general debility, premature decrepitude. Scarcely is there one to whom you put the question, who has not, in the course of his life, brought upon himself illnesses which a little information would have saved him from. Here is a case of heart-disease consequent on a rheumatic fever that followed reckless exposure. There is a case of eyes spoiled for life by over-study. Yesterday the account was of one whose long-enduring lameness was brought on by continuing, spite of the pain, to use a knee after it had been slightly injured. And to-day we are told of another who has had to lie by for years, because he did not know that the palpitation he suffered under resulted from overtaxed brain. Now we hear of an irremediable injury which followed some silly feat of strength; and, again, of a constitution that has never recovered from the effects of excessive work needlessly undertaken. While on every side we see the perpetual minor ailments which accompany feebleness. Not to dwell on the pain, the weariness, the gloom, the waste of time and money thus entailed, only consider how greatly ill-health hinders the discharge of all duties—makes business often impossible, and always more difficult; produces an irritability fatal to the right management of children; puts the functions of citizenship out of the question; and makes amusement a bore. Is it not clear that the physical sins—partly our forefathers' and partly our own—which produce this ill-health, deduct more from complete living than anything else? and to a great extent make life a failure and a burden instead of a benefaction and a pleasure?

Nor is this all. Life, besides being thus immensely deteriorated, is also cut short. It is not true, as we commonly suppose, that after a disorder or disease from which we have recovered, we are as before. No disturbance of the normal course of the functions can pass away and leave things exactly as they were. A permanent damage is done—not immediately appreciable, it may be, but still there; and along with other such items which Nature in her strict account-keeping never drops, it will tell against us to the inevitable shortening of our days. Through the accumulation of small injuries it is that constitutions are commonly undermined, and break down, long before their time. And if we call to mind how far the average duration of life falls below the possible duration, we see how immense is the loss. When, to the numerous partial deductions which bad health entails, we add this great final deduction, it results that ordinarily one-half of life is thrown away.

Hence, knowledge which subserves direct self-preservation by preventing this loss of health, is of primary importance. We do not contend that possession of such knowledge would by any means wholly remedy the evil. It is clear that in our present phase of civilisation, men's necessities often compel them to transgress. And it is further clear that, even in the absence of such compulsion, their inclinations would frequently lead them, spite of their convictions, to sacrifice future good to present gratification. But we *do* contend that the right knowledge impressed in the right way would effect much; and we further contend that as the laws of health must be recognised before they can be fully conformed to, the imparting of such knowledge must precede a more rational living—come when that may. We infer that as vigorous health and its accompanying high spirits are larger elements of happiness than any other things whatever, the teaching how to maintain them is a teaching that yields in moment to no other whatever. And therefore we assert that such a course of physiology as is needful for the comprehension of its general truths, and their bearings on daily conduct, is an all-essential part of a rational education.

Strange that the assertion should need making! Stranger still that it should need defending! Yet are there not a few by whom such a proposition will be received with something approaching to derision. Men who would blush if caught saying Iphigénia instead of Iphigenía, or would resent as an insult any imputation of ignorance respecting the fabled labours of a fabled demi-god, show not the slightest shame in confessing that they do not know where the Eustachian tubes are, what are the actions of the spinal cord, what is the normal rate of pulsation, or how the lungs are inflated. While anxious that their sons should be well up in the superstitions of two thousand years ago, they care not that they should be taught anything about the structure and functions of their own bodies—nay, even wish them not to be so taught. So overwhelming is the influence of established routine! So terribly in our education does the ornamental over-ride the useful!

We need not insist on the value of that knowledge which aids indirect self-preservation by facilitating the gaining of a livelihood. This is admitted by all; and, indeed, by the mass is perhaps too exclusively regarded as the end of education. But while every one is ready to endorse the abstract proposition that instruction fitting youths for the business of life is of high importance, or even to consider it of supreme importance; yet scarcely any inquire what instruction will so fit them. It is true that reading, writing, and arithmetic are taught with an intelligent appreciation of their uses. But when we have said this we have said nearly all. While the great bulk of what else is acquired has no bearing on the industrial activities, an immensity of information that has a direct bearing on the industrial activities is entirely passed over.

For, leaving out only some very small classes, what are all men employed in? They are employed in the production, preparation, and distribution of commodities. And on what does efficiency in the production, preparation, and distribution of commodities depend? It depends on the use of methods fitted to the respective natures of these commodities; it depends on an adequate acquaintance with their physical, chemical, or vital properties, as the case may be; that is, it depends on Science. This order of knowledge which is in great part ignored in our school-courses, is the order of knowledge underlying the right performance of those processes by which civilised life is made possible. Undeniable as is this truth, there seems to be no living consciousness of it: its very familiarity makes it unregarded. To give due weight to our argument, we must, therefore, realise this truth to the reader by a rapid review of the facts.

Passing over the most abstract science, Logic, on the due guidance by which, however, the large producer or distributor depends, knowingly or unknowingly, for success in his business-forecasts, we come first to Mathematics. Of this, the most general division, dealing with number, guides all industrial activities; be they those by which processes are adjusted, or estimates framed, or commodities bought and sold, or accounts kept. No one needs to have the value of this division of abstract science insisted upon.

For the higher arts of construction, some acquaintance with the more special division of Mathematics is indispensable. The village carpenter, who lays out his work by empirical rules, equally with the builder of a Britannia Bridge, makes hourly reference to the laws of space-relations. The surveyor who measures the land purchased; the architect in designing a mansion to be built on it; the builder when laying out the foundations; the masons in cutting the stones; and the various artizans who put up the fittings; are all guided by geometrical truths. Railway-making is regulated from beginning to end by geometry: alike in the preparation of plans and sections; in staking out the line; in the mensuration of cuttings and embankments; in the designing and building of bridges, culverts, viaducts, tunnels, stations. Similarly with the harbours, docks, piers, and various engineering and architectural works that fringe the coasts and overspread the country, as well as the mines that run underneath it. And now-a-days, even the farmer, for the correct laying-out of his drains, has recourse to the level—that is, to geometrical principles.

Turn next to the Abstract-Concrete sciences. On the application of the simplest of these, Mechanics, depends the success of modern manufactures. The properties of the lever, the wheel-and-axle, etc., are recognised in every machine, and to machinery in these times we owe all production. Trace the history of the breakfast-roll. The soil out of which it came was drained with machine-made tiles; the surface was turned over by a machine; the wheat was reaped, thrashed, and winnowed by machines; by machinery it was ground and bolted; and had the flour been sent to Gosport, it might have been made into biscuits by a machine. Look round the room in which you sit. If modern, probably the bricks in its walls were machine-made; and by machinery the flooring was sawn and planed, the mantel-shelf sawn and polished, the paper-hangings made and printed. The veneer on the table, the turned legs of the chairs, the carpet, the curtains, are all products of machinery. Your clothing—plain, figured, or printed—is it not wholly woven, nay, perhaps even sewed, by machinery? And the volume you are reading—are not its leaves fabricated by one machine and covered with these words by another? Add to which that for the means of distribution over both land and sea, we are similarly indebted. And then observe that according as knowledge of mechanics is well or ill applied to these ends, comes success or failure. The engineer who miscalculates the strength of materials, builds a bridge that breaks down. The manufacturer who uses a bad machine cannot compete with another whose machine wastes less in friction and inertia. The ship-builder adhering to the old model is out-sailed by one who builds on the mechanically-justified wave-line principle. And as the ability of a nation to hold its own against other nations, depends on the skilled activity of its units, we see that on mechanical knowledge may turn the national fate.

On ascending from the divisions of Abstract-Concrete science dealing with molar forces, to those divisions of it which deal with molecular forces, we come to another vast series of applications. To this group of sciences joined with the preceding groups we owe the steam-engine, which does the work of millions of labourers. That section of physics which formulates the laws of heat, has taught us how to economise fuel in various industries; how to increase the produce of smelting furnaces by substituting the hot for the cold blast; how to ventilate mines; how to prevent explosions by using the safety-lamp; and, through the thermometer, how to regulate innumerable processes. That section which has the phenomena of light for its subject, gives eyes to the old and the myopic; aids through the microscope in detecting diseases and adulterations; and, by improved lighthouses, prevents shipwrecks. Researches in electricity and magnetism have saved innumerable lives and incalculable property through the compass; have subserved many arts by the electrotype; and now, in the telegraph, have supplied us with an agency by which for the future, mercantile transactions will be regulated and political intercourse carried on. While in the details of in-door life, from the improved kitchen-range up to the stereoscope on the drawing-room table, the applications of advanced physics underlie our comforts and gratifications.

Still more numerous are the applications of Chemistry. The bleacher, the dyer, the calico-printer, are severally occupied in processes that are well or ill done according as they do or do not conform to chemical laws. Smelting of copper, tin, zinc, lead, silver, iron, must be guided by chemistry. Sugar-refining, gas-making, soap-boiling, gunpowder-manufacture, are operations all partly chemical; as are likewise those which produce glass and porcelain. Whether the distiller's wort stops at the alcoholic fermentation or passes into the acetous, is a chemical question on which hangs his profit or loss; and the brewer, if his business is extensive, finds it pay to keep a chemist on his premises. Indeed, there is now scarcely any manufacture over some part of which chemistry does not preside. Nay, in these times even agriculture, to be profitably carried on, must have like guidance. The analysis of manures and soils; the disclosure of their respective adaptations; the use of gypsum or other substance for fixing ammonia; the utilisation of coprolites; the production of artificial manures—all these are boons of chemistry which it behoves the farmer to acquaint himself with. Be it in the lucifer match, or in disinfected sewage, or in photographs—in bread made without fermentation, or perfumes extracted from refuse, we may perceive that chemistry affects all our industries; and that, therefore, knowledge of it concerns every one who is directly or indirectly connected with our industries.

Of the Concrete sciences, we come first to Astronomy. Out of this has grown that art of navigation which has made possible the enormous foreign commerce that supports a large part of our population, while supplying us with many necessaries and most of our luxuries.

Geology, again, is a science knowledge of which greatly aids industrial success. Now that iron ores are so large a source of wealth; now that the duration of our coal-supply has become a question of great interest; now that we have a College of Mines and a Geological Survey; it is scarcely needful to enlarge on the truth that the study of the Earth's crust is important to our material welfare.

And then the science of life—Biology: does not this, too, bear fundamentally on these processes of indirect self-preservation? With what we ordinarily call manufactures, it has, indeed, little connection; but with the all-essential manufacture—that of food—it is inseparably connected. As agriculture must conform its methods to the phenomena of vegetal and animal life, it follows that the science of these phenomena is the rational basis of agriculture. Various biological truths have indeed been empirically established and acted upon by farmers, while yet there has been no conception of them as science; such as that particular manures are suited to particular plants; that crops of certain kinds unfit the soil for other crops; that horses cannot do good work on poor food; that such and such diseases of cattle and sheep are caused by such and such conditions. These, and the every-day knowledge which the agriculturist gains by experience respecting the management of plants and animals, constitute his stock of biological facts; on the largeness of which greatly depends his success. And as these biological facts, scanty, indefinite, rudimentary, though they are, aid him so essentially; judge what must be the value to him of such facts when they become positive, definite, and exhaustive. Indeed, even now we may see the benefits that rational biology is conferring on him. The truth that the production of animal heat implies waste of substance, and that, therefore, preventing loss of heat prevents the need for extra food—a purely theoretical conclusion—now guides the fattening of cattle: it is found that by keeping cattle warm, fodder is saved. Similarly with respect to variety of food. The experiments of physiologists have shown that not only is change of diet beneficial, but that digestion is facilitated by a mixture of ingredients in each meal. The discovery that a disorder known as "the staggers," of which many thousands of sheep have died annually, is caused by an entozoon which presses on the brain, and that if the creature is extracted through the softened place in the skull which marks its position, the sheep usually recovers, is another debt which agriculture owes to biology.

Yet one more science have we to note as bearing directly on industrial success—the Science of Society. Men who daily look at the state of the money-market glance over prices current; discuss the probable crops of corn, cotton, sugar, wool, silk; weigh the chances of war; and from these data decide on their mercantile operations; are students of social science: empirical and blundering students it may be; but still, students who gain the prizes or are plucked of their profits, according as they do or do not reach the right conclusion. Not only the manufacturer and the merchant must guide their transactions by calculations of supply and demand, based on numerous facts, and tacitly recognising sundry general principles of social action; but even the retailer must do the like: his prosperity very greatly depending upon the correctness of his judgments respecting the future wholesale prices and the future rates of consumption. Manifestly, whoever takes part in the entangled commercial activities of a community, is vitally interested in understanding the laws according to which those activities vary.

Thus, to all such as are occupied in the production, exchange, or distribution of commodities, acquaintance with Science in some of its departments, is of fundamental importance. Each man who is immediately or remotely implicated in any form of industry and few are not has in some way to deal with the mathematical, physical, and chemical properties of things; perhaps, also, has a direct interest in biology; and certainly has in sociology. Whether he does or does not succeed well in that indirect self-preservation which we call getting a good livelihood, depends in a great degree on his knowledge of one or more of these sciences: not, it may be, a rational knowledge; but still a knowledge, though empirical. For what we call learning a business, really implies learning the science involved in it; though not perhaps under the name of science. And hence a grounding in science is of great importance, both because it prepares for all this, and because rational knowledge has an immense superiority over empirical knowledge. Moreover, not only is scientific culture requisite for each, that he may understand the *how* and the *why* of the things and processes with which he is concerned as maker or distributor; but it is often of much moment that he should understand the *how* and the *why* of various other things and processes. In this age of joint-stock undertakings, nearly every man above the labourer is interested as capitalist in some other occupation than his own; and, as thus interested, his profit or loss often depends on his knowledge of the sciences bearing on this other occupation. Here is a mine, in the sinking of which many shareholders ruined themselves, from not knowing that a certain fossil belonged to the old red sandstone, below which no coal is found. Numerous attempts have been made to construct electromagnetic engines, in the hope of superseding steam; but had those who supplied the money understood the general law of the correlation and equivalence of forces, they might have had better balances at their bankers. Daily are men induced to aid in carrying out inventions which a mere tyro in science could show to be futile. Scarcely a locality but has its history of fortunes thrown away over some impossible project.

And if already the loss from want of science is so frequent and so great, still greater and more frequent will it be to those who hereafter lack science. Just as fast as productive processes become more scientific, which competition will inevitably make them do; and just as fast as joint-stock undertakings spread, which they certainly will; so fast must scientific knowledge grow necessary to every one.

That which our school-courses leave almost entirely out, we thus find to be that which most nearly concerns the business of life. Our industries would cease, were it not for the information which men begin to acquire, as they best may, after their education is said to be finished. And were it not for this information, from age to age accumulated and spread by unofficial means, these industries would never have existed. Had there been no teaching but such as goes on in our public schools, England would now be what it was in feudal times. That increasing acquaintance with the laws of phenomena, which has through successive ages enabled us to subjugate Nature to our needs, and in these days gives the common labourer comforts which a few centuries ago kings could not purchase, is scarcely in any degree owed to the appointed means of instructing our youth. The vital knowledge—that by which we have grown as a nation to what we are, and which now underlies our whole existence, is a knowledge that has got itself taught in nooks and corners; while the ordained agencies for teaching have been mumbling little else but dead formulas.

We come now to the third great division of human activities—a division for which no preparation whatever is made. If by some strange chance not a vestige of us descended to the remote future save a pile of our school-books or some college examination papers, we may imagine how puzzled an antiquary of the period would be on finding in them no sign that the learners were ever likely to be parents. "This must have been the *curriculum* for their celibates," we may fancy him concluding. "I perceive here an elaborate preparation for many things; especially for reading the books of extinct nations and of co-existing nations from which indeed it seems clear that these people had very little worth reading in their own tongue; but I find no reference whatever to the bringing up of children. They could not have been so absurd as to omit all training for this gravest of responsibilities. Evidently then, this was the school-course of one of their monastic orders."

Seriously, is it not an astonishing fact, that though on the treatment of offspring depend their lives or deaths, and their moral welfare or ruin; yet not one word of instruction on the treatment of offspring is ever given to those who will by and by be parents? Is it not monstrous that the fate of a new generation should be left to the chances of unreasoning custom, impulse, fancy—joined with the suggestions of ignorant nurses and the prejudiced counsel of grandmothers? If a merchant commenced business without any knowledge of arithmetic and book-keeping, we should exclaim at his folly, and look for disastrous consequences. Or if, before studying anatomy, a man set up as a surgical operator, we should wonder at his audacity and pity his patients. But that parents should begin the difficult task of rearing children, without ever having given a thought to the principles—physical, moral, or intellectual—which ought to guide them, excites neither surprise at the actors nor pity for their victims.

To tens of thousands that are killed, add hundreds of thousand that survive with feeble constitutions, and millions that grow up with constitutions not so strong as they should be; and you will have some idea of the curse inflicted on their offspring by parents ignorant of the laws of life. Do but consider for a moment that the regimen to which children are subject, is hourly telling upon them to their life-long injury or benefit; and that there are twenty ways of going wrong to one way of going right; and you will get some idea of the enormous mischief that is almost everywhere inflicted by the thoughtless, haphazard system in common use. Is it decided that a boy shall be clothed in some flimsy short dress, and be allowed to go playing about with limbs reddened by cold? The decision will tell on his whole future existence—either in illnesses; or in stunted growth; or in deficient energy; or in a maturity less vigorous than it ought to have been, and in consequent hindrances to success and happiness. Are children doomed to a monotonous dietary, or a dietary that is deficient in nutritiveness? Their ultimate physical power, and their efficiency as men and women, will inevitably be more or less diminished by it. Are they forbidden vociferous play, or being too ill-clothed to bear exposure are they kept indoors in cold weather? They are certain to fall below that measure of health and strength to which they would else have attained. When sons and daughters grow up sickly and feeble, parents commonly regard the event as a misfortune—as a visitation of Providence. Thinking after the prevalent chaotic fashion, they assume that these evils come without causes; or that the causes are supernatural. Nothing of the kind. In some cases the causes are doubtless inherited; but in most cases foolish regulations are the causes. Very generally, parents themselves are responsible for all this pain, this debility, this depression, this misery. They have undertaken to control the lives of their offspring from hour to hour; with cruel carelessness they have neglected to learn anything about these vital processes which they are unceasingly affecting by their commands and prohibitions; in utter ignorance of the simplest physiologic laws, they have been year by year undermining the constitutions of their children; and have so inflicted disease and premature death, not only on them but on their descendants.

Equally great are the ignorance and the consequent injury, when we turn from physical training to moral training. Consider the young mother and her nursery-legislation. But a few years ago she was at school, where her memory was crammed with words, and names, and dates, and her reflective faculties scarcely in the slightest degree exercised—where not one idea was given her respecting the methods of dealing with the opening mind of childhood; and where her discipline did not in the least fit her for thinking out methods of her own. The intervening years have been passed in practising music, in fancy-work, in novel-reading, and in party-going: no thought having yet been given to the grave responsibilities of maternity; and scarcely any of that solid intellectual culture obtained which would be some preparation for such responsibilities. And now see her with an unfolding human character committed to her charge—see her profoundly ignorant of the phenomena with which she has to deal, undertaking to do that which can be done but imperfectly even with the aid of the profoundest knowledge. She knows nothing about the nature of the emotions, their order of evolution, their functions, or where use ends and abuse begins. She is under the impression that some of the feelings are wholly bad, which is not true of any one of them; and that others are good however far they may be carried, which is also not true of any one of them. And then, ignorant as she is of the structure she has to deal with, she is equally ignorant of the effects produced on it by this or that treatment. What can be more inevitable than the disastrous results we see hourly arising? Lacking knowledge of mental phenomena, with their cause and consequences, her interference is frequently more mischievous than absolute passivity would have been. This and that kind of action, which are quite normal and beneficial, she perpetually thwarts; and so diminishes the child's happiness and profit, injures its temper and her own, and produces estrangement. Deeds which she thinks it desirable to encourage, she gets performed by threats and bribes, or by exciting a desire for applause: considering little what the inward motive may be, so long as the outward conduct conforms; and thus cultivating hypocrisy, and fear, and selfishness, in place of good feeling. While insisting on truthfulness, she constantly sets an example of untruth by threatening penalties which she does not inflict. While inculcating self-control, she hourly visits on her little ones angry scoldings for acts undeserving of them. She has not the remotest idea that in the nursery, as in the world, that alone is the truly salutary discipline which visits on all conduct, good and bad, the natural consequences—the consequences, pleasurable or painful, which in the nature of things such conduct tends to bring. Being thus without theoretic guidance, and quite incapable of guiding herself by tracing the mental processes going on in her children, her rule is impulsive, inconsistent, mischievous; and would indeed be generally ruinous were it not that the overwhelming tendency of the growing mind to assume the moral type of the race usually subordinates all minor influences.

And then the culture of the intellect—is not this, too, mismanaged in a similar manner? Grant that the phenomena of intelligence conform to laws; grant that the evolution of intelligence in a child also conforms to laws; and it follows inevitably that education cannot be rightly guided without a knowledge of these laws. To suppose that you can properly regulate this process of forming and accumulating ideas, without understanding the nature of the process, is absurd. How widely, then, must teaching as it is differ from teaching as it should be; when hardly any parents, and but few tutors, know anything about psychology. As might be expected, the established system is grievously at fault, alike in matter and in manner. While the right class of facts is withheld, the wrong class is forcibly administered in the wrong way and in the wrong order. Under that common limited idea of education which confines it to knowledge gained from books, parents thrust primers into the hands of their little ones years too soon, to their great injury. Not recognising the truth that the function of books is supplementary—that they form an indirect means to knowledge when direct means fail—a means of seeing through other men what you cannot see for yourself; teachers are eager to give second-hand facts in place of first-hand facts. Not perceiving the enormous value of that spontaneous education which goes on in early years—not perceiving that a child's restless observation, instead of being ignored or checked, should be diligently ministered to, and made as accurate and complete as possible; they insist on occupying its eyes and thoughts with things that are, for the time being, incomprehensible and repugnant. Possessed by a superstition which worships the symbols of knowledge instead of the knowledge itself, they do not see that only when his acquaintance with the objects and processes of the household, the streets, and the fields, is becoming tolerably exhaustive—only then should a child be introduced to the new sources of information which books supply: and this, not only because immediate cognition is of far greater value than mediate cognition; but also, because the words contained in books can be rightly interpreted into ideas, only in proportion to the antecedent experience of things. Observe next, that this formal instruction, far too soon commenced, is carried on with but little reference to the laws of mental development.

Intellectual progress is of necessity from the concrete to the abstract. But regardless of this, highly abstract studies, such as grammar, which should come quite late, are begun quite early. Political geography, dead and uninteresting to a child, and which should be an appendage of sociological studies, is commenced betimes; while physical geography, comprehensible and comparatively attractive to a child, is in great part passed over. Nearly every subject dealt with is arranged in abnormal order: definitions and rules and principles being put first, instead of being disclosed, as they are in the order of nature, through the study of cases. And then, pervading the whole, is the vicious system of rote learning—a system of sacrificing the spirit to the letter. See the results. What with perceptions unnaturally dulled by early thwarting, and a coerced attention to books—what with the mental confusion produced by teaching subjects before they can be understood, and in each of them giving generalisations before the facts of which they are the generalisations—what with making the pupil a mere passive recipient of other's ideas, and not in the least leading him to be an active inquirer or self-instructor—and what with taxing the faculties to excess; there are very few minds that become as efficient as they might be. Examinations being once passed, books are laid aside; the greater part of what has been acquired, being unorganised, soon drops out of recollection; what remains is mostly inert—the art of applying knowledge not having been cultivated; and there is but little power either of accurate observation or independent thinking. To all which add, that while much of the information gained is of relatively small value, an immense mass of information of transcendent value is entirely passed over.

Thus we find the facts to be such as might have been inferred *à priori*. The training of children—physical, moral, and intellectual—is dreadfully defective. And in great measure it is so because parents are devoid of that knowledge by which this training can alone be rightly guided. What is to be expected when one of the most intricate of problems is undertaken by those who have given scarcely a thought to the principles on which its solution depends? For shoe-making or house-building, for the management of a ship or a locomotive engine, a long apprenticeship is needful. Is it, then, that the unfolding of a human being in body and mind is so comparatively simple a process that any one may superintend and regulate it with no preparation whatever? If not—if the process is, with one exception, more complex than any in Nature, and the task of ministering to it one of surpassing difficulty; is it not madness to make no provision for such a task? Better sacrifice accomplishments than omit this all-essential instruction. When a father, acting on false dogmas adopted without examination, has alienated his sons, driven them into rebellion by his harsh treatment, ruined them, and made himself miserable; he might reflect that the study of Ethology would have been worth pursuing, even at the cost of knowing nothing about Æschylus. When a mother is mourning over a first-born that has sunk under the sequelæ of scarlet-fever—when perhaps a candid medical man has confirmed her suspicion that her child would have recovered had not its system been enfeebled by over-study—when she is prostrate under the pangs of combined grief and remorse; it is but a small consolation that she can read Dante in the original.

Thus we see that for regulating the third great division of human activities, a knowledge of the laws of life is the one thing needful. Some acquaintance with the first principles of physiology and the elementary truths of psychology, is indispensable for the right bringing up of children. We doubt not that many will read this assertion with a smile. That parents in general should be expected to acquire a knowledge of subjects so abstruse will seem to them an absurdity. And if we proposed that an exhaustive knowledge of these subjects should be obtained by all fathers and mothers, the absurdity would indeed be glaring enough. But we do not. General principles only, accompanied by such illustrations as may be needed to make them understood, would suffice. And these might be readily taught—if not rationally, then dogmatically. Be this as it may, however, here are the indisputable facts:—that the development of children in mind and body follows certain laws; that unless these laws are in some degree conformed to by parents, death is inevitable; that unless they are in a great degree conformed to, there must result serious physical and mental defects; and that only when they are completely conformed to, can a perfect maturity be reached. Judge, then, whether all who may one day be parents, should not strive with some anxiety to learn what these laws are.

From the parental functions let us pass now to the functions of the citizen. We have here to inquire what knowledge fits a man for the discharge of these functions. It cannot be alleged that the need for knowledge fitting him for these functions is wholly overlooked; for our school-courses contain certain studies, which, nominally at least, bear upon political and social duties. Of these the only one that occupies a prominent place is History.

But, as already hinted, the information commonly given under this head, is almost valueless for purposes of guidance. Scarcely any of the facts set down in our school-histories, and very few of those contained in the more elaborate works written for adults, illustrate the right principles of political action. The biographies of monarchs and our children learn little else throw scarcely any light upon the science of society. Familiarity with court intrigues, plots, usurpations, or the like, and with all the personalities accompanying them, aids very little in elucidating the causes of national progress. We read of some squabble for power, that it led to a pitched battle; that such and such were the names of the generals and their leading subordinates; that they had each so many thousand infantry and cavalry, and so many cannon; that they arranged their forces in this and that order; that they manœuvred, attacked, and fell back in certain ways; that at this part of the day such disasters were sustained, and at that such advantages gained; that in one particular movement some leading officer fell, while in another a certain regiment was decimated; that after all the changing fortunes of the fight, the victory was gained by this or that army; and that so many were killed and wounded on each side, and so many captured by the conquerors. And now, out of the accumulated details making up the narrative, say which it is that helps you in deciding on your conduct as a citizen. Supposing even that you had diligently read, not only *The Fifteen Decisive Battles of the World*, but accounts of all other battles that history mentions; how much more judicious would your vote be at the next election? "But these are facts—interesting facts," you say. Without doubt they are facts such, at least, as are not wholly or partially fictions; and to many they may be interesting facts. But this by no means implies that they are valuable. Factitious or morbid opinion often gives seeming value to things that have scarcely any. A tulipomaniac will not part with a choice bulb for its weight in gold. To another man an ugly piece of cracked old china seems his most desirable possession. And there are those who give high prices for the relics of celebrated murderers. Will it be contended that these tastes are any measures of value in the things that gratify them? If not, then it must be admitted that the liking felt for certain classes of historical facts is no proof of their worth; and that we must test their worth, as we test the worth of other facts, by asking to what uses they are applicable. Were some one to tell you that your neighbour's cat kittened yesterday, you would say the information was valueless. Fact though it might be, you would call it an utterly useless fact—a fact that could in no way influence your actions in life—a fact that would not help you in learning how to live completely. Well, apply the same test to the great mass of historical facts, and you will get the same result. They are facts from which no conclusions can be drawn—*unorganisable* facts; and therefore facts of no service in establishing principles of conduct, which is the chief use of facts. Read them, if you like, for amusement; but do not flatter your self they are instructive.

That which constitutes History, properly so called, is in great part omitted from works on the subject. Only of late years have historians commenced giving us, in any considerable quantity, the truly valuable information. As in past ages the king was everything and the people nothing; so, in past histories the doings of the king fill the entire picture, to which the national life forms but an obscure background. While only now, when the welfare of nations rather than of rulers is becoming the dominant idea, are historians beginning to occupy themselves with the phenomena of social progress. The thing it really concerns us to know is the natural history of society. We want all facts which help us to understand how a nation has grown and organised itself. Among these, let us of course have an account of its government; with as little as may be of gossip about the men who officered it, and as much as possible about the structure, principles, methods, prejudices, corruptions, etc., which it exhibited: and let this account include not only the nature and actions of the central government, but also those of local governments, down to their minutest ramifications. Let us of course also have a parallel description of the ecclesiastical government—its organisation, its conduct, its power, its relations to the State; and accompanying this, the ceremonial, creed, and religious ideas—not only those nominally believed, but those really believed and acted upon. Let us at the same time be informed of the control exercised by class over class, as displayed in social observances—in titles, salutations, and forms of address. Let us know, too, what were all the other customs which regulated the popular life out of doors and in-doors: including those concerning the relations of the sexes, and the relations of parents to children. The superstitions, also, from the more important myths down to the charms in common use, should be indicated. Next should come a delineation of the industrial system: showing to what extent the division of labour was carried; how trades were regulated, whether by caste, guilds, or otherwise; what was the connection between employers and employed; what were the agencies for distributing commodities; what were the means of communication; what was the circulating medium. Accompanying all which should be given an account of the industrial arts technically considered: stating the processes in use, and the quality of the products. Further, the intellectual condition of the nation in its various grades should be depicted; not only with respect to the kind and amount of education, but with respect to the progress made in science, and the prevailing manner of thinking. The degree of æsthetic culture, as displayed in architecture, sculpture, painting, dress, music, poetry, and fiction, should be described. Nor should there be omitted a sketch of the daily lives of the people—their food, their homes, and their amusements. And lastly, to connect the whole, should be exhibited the morals, theoretical and practical, of all classes: as indicated in their laws, habits, proverbs, deeds. These facts, given with as much brevity as consists with clearness and accuracy, should be so grouped and arranged that they may be comprehended in their *ensemble*, and contemplated as mutually-dependent parts of one great whole. The aim should be so to present them that men may readily trace the *consensus* subsisting among them; with the view of learning what social phenomena co-exist with what other. And then the corresponding delineations of succeeding ages should be so managed as to show how each belief, institution, custom, and arrangement was modified; and how the *consensus* of preceding structures and functions was developed into the *consensus* of succeeding ones. Such alone is the kind of information respecting past times which can be of service to the citizen for the regulation of his conduct. The only history that is of practical value is what may be called Descriptive Sociology. And the highest office which the historian can discharge, is that of so narrating the lives of nations, as to furnish materials for a Comparative Sociology; and for the subsequent determination of the ultimate laws to which social phenomena conform.

But now mark, that even supposing an adequate stock of this truly valuable historical knowledge has been acquired, it is of comparatively little use without the key. And the key is to be found only in Science. In the absence of the generalisations of biology and psychology, rational interpretation of social phenomena is impossible. Only in proportion as men draw certain rude, empirical inferences respecting human nature, are they enabled to understand even the simplest facts of social life: as, for instance, the relation between supply and demand. And if the most elementary truths of sociology cannot be reached until some knowledge is obtained of how men generally think, feel, and act under given circumstances; then it is manifest that there can be nothing like a wide comprehension of sociology, unless through a competent acquaintance with man in all his faculties, bodily, and mental. Consider the matter in the abstract, and this conclusion is self-evident. Thus:—Society is made up of individuals; all that is done in society is done by the combined actions of individuals; and therefore, in individual actions only can be found the solutions of social phenomena. But the actions of individuals depend on the laws of their natures; and their actions cannot be understood until these laws are understood. These laws, however, when reduced to their simplest expressions, prove to be corollaries from the laws of body and mind in general. Hence it follows, that biology and psychology are indispensable as interpreters of sociology. Or, to state the conclusions still more simply:—all social phenomena are phenomena of life—are the most complex manifestations of life—must conform to the laws of life—and can be understood only when the laws of life are understood. Thus, then, for the regulation of this fourth division of human activities, we are, as before, dependent on Science. Of the knowledge commonly imparted in educational courses, very little is of service for guiding a man in his conduct as a citizen. Only a small part of the history he reads is of practical value; and of this small part he is not prepared to make proper use. He lacks not only the materials for, but the very conception of, descriptive sociology; and he also lacks those generalisations of the organic sciences, without which even descriptive sociology can give him but small aid.

And now we come to that remaining division of human life which includes the relaxations and amusements filling leisure hours. After considering what training best fits for self-preservation, for the obtainment of sustenance, for the discharge of parental duties, and for the regulation of social and political conduct; we have now to consider what training best fits for the miscellaneous ends not included in these—for the enjoyment of Nature, of Literature, and of the Fine Arts, in all their forms. Postponing them as we do to things that bear more vitally upon human welfare; and bringing everything, as we have, to the test of actual value; it will perhaps be inferred that we are inclined to slight these less essential things. No greater mistake could be made, however. We yield to none in the value we attach to aesthetic culture and its pleasures. Without painting, sculpture, music, poetry, and the emotions produced by natural beauty of every kind, life would lose half its charm. So far from regarding the training and gratification of the tastes as unimportant, we believe that in time to come they will occupy a much larger share of human life than now. When the forces of Nature have been fully conquered to man's use—when the means of production have been brought to perfection—when labour has been economised to the highest degree—when education has been so systematised that a preparation for the more essential activities may be made with comparative rapidity—and when, consequently, there is a great increase of spare time; then will the beautiful, both in Art and Nature, rightly fill a large space in the minds of all.

But it is one thing to approve of æsthetic culture as largely conducive to human happiness; and another thing to admit that it is a fundamental requisite to human happiness. However important it may be, it must yield precedence to those kinds of culture which bear directly upon daily duties. As before hinted, literature and the fine arts are made possible by those activities which make individual and social life possible; and manifestly, that which is made possible, must be postponed to that which makes it possible. A florist cultivates a plant for the sake of its flower; and regards the roots and leaves as of value, chiefly because they are instrumental in producing the flower. But while, as an ultimate product, the flower is the thing to which everything else is subordinate, the florist has learnt that the root and leaves are intrinsically of greater importance; because on them the evolution of the flower depends. He bestows every care in rearing a healthy plant; and knows it would be folly if, in his anxiety to obtain the flower, he were to neglect the plant. Similarly in the case before us. Architecture, sculpture, painting, music, and poetry, may truly be called the efflorescence of civilised life. But even supposing they are of such transcendent worth as to subordinate the civilised life out of which they grow which can hardly be asserted, it will still be admitted that the production of a healthy civilised life must be the first consideration; and that culture subserving this must occupy the highest place.

And here we see most distinctly the vice of our educational system. It neglects the plant for the sake of the flower. In anxiety for elegance, it forgets substance. While it gives no knowledge conducive to self-preservation—while of knowledge that facilitates gaining a livelihood it gives but the rudiments, and leaves the greater part to be picked up any how in after life—while for the discharge of parental functions it makes not the slightest provision—and while for the duties of citizenship it prepares by imparting a mass of facts, most of which are irrelevant, and the rest without a key; it is diligent in teaching whatever adds to refinement, polish, éclat. Fully as we may admit that extensive acquaintance with modern languages is a valuable accomplishment, which, through reading, conversation, and travel, aids in giving a certain finish; it by no means follows that this result is rightly purchased at the cost of the vitally important knowledge sacrificed to it. Supposing it true that classical education conduces to elegance and correctness of style; it cannot be said that elegance and correctness of style are comparable in importance to a familiarity with the principles that should guide the rearing of children. Grant that the taste may be improved by reading the poetry written in extinct languages; yet it is not to be inferred that such improvement of taste is equivalent in value to an acquaintance with the laws of health. Accomplishments, the fine arts, *belles-lettres*, and all those things which, as we say, constitute the efflorescence of civilisation, should be wholly subordinate to that instruction and discipline in which civilisation rests. *As they occupy the leisure part of life, so should they occupy the leisure part of education.*

Recognising thus the true position of aesthetics, and holding that while the cultivation of them should form a part of education from its commencement, such cultivation should be subsidiary; we have now to inquire what knowledge is of most use to this end—what knowledge best fits for this remaining sphere of activity? To this question the answer is still the same as heretofore. Unexpected though the assertion may be, it is nevertheless true, that the highest Art of every kind is based on Science—that without Science there can be neither perfect production nor full appreciation. Science, in that limited acceptation current in society, may not have been possessed by various artists of high repute; but acute observers as such artists have been, they have always possessed a stock of those empirical generalisations which constitute science in its lowest phase; and they have habitually fallen far below perfection, partly because their generalisations were comparatively few and inaccurate. That science necessarily underlies the fine arts, becomes manifest, *à priori*, when we remember that art-products are all more or less representative of objective or subjective phenomena; that they can be good only in proportion as they conform to the laws of these phenomena; and that before they can thus conform, the artist must know what these laws are. That this *à priori* conclusion tallies with experience, we shall soon see.

Youths preparing for the practice of sculpture have to acquaint themselves with the bones and muscles of the human frame in their distribution, attachments, and movements. This is a portion of science; and it has been found needful to impart it for the prevention of those many errors which sculptors who do not possess it commit. A knowledge of mechanical principles is also requisite; and such knowledge not being usually possessed, grave mechanical mistakes are frequently made. Take an instance. For the stability of a figure it is needful that the perpendicular from the centre of gravity—"the line of direction," as it is called—should fall within the base of support; and hence it happens, that when a man assumes the attitude known as "standing at ease," in which one leg is straightened and the other relaxed, the line of direction falls within the foot of the straightened leg. But sculptors unfamiliar with the theory of equilibrium, not uncommonly so represent this attitude, that the line of direction falls midway between the feet. Ignorance of the law of momentum leads to analogous blunders: as witness the admired Discobolus, which, as it is posed, must inevitably fall forward the moment the quoit is delivered.

In painting, the necessity for scientific information, empirical if not rational, is still more conspicuous. What gives the grotesqueness of Chinese pictures, unless their utter disregard of the laws of appearances—their absurd linear perspective, and their want of aerial perspective? In what are the drawings of a child so faulty, if not in a similar absence of truth—an absence arising, in great part, from ignorance of the way in which the aspects of things vary with the conditions? Do but remember the books and lectures by which students are instructed; or consider the criticisms of Ruskin; or look at the doings of the Pre-Raffaelites; and you will see that progress in painting implies increasing knowledge of how effects in Nature are produced. The most diligent observation, if unaided by science, fails to preserve from error. Every painter will endorse the assertion that unless it is known what appearances must exist under given circumstances, they often will not be perceived; and to know what appearances must exist, is, in so far, to understand the science of appearances. From want of science Mr. J. Lewis, careful painter as he is, casts the shadow of a lattice-window in sharply-defined lines upon an opposite wall; which he would not have done, had he been familiar with the phenomena of penumbræ. From want of science, Mr. Rosetti, catching sight of a peculiar iridescence displayed by certain hairy surfaces under particular lights an iridescence caused by the diffraction of light in passing the hairs, commits the error of showing this iridescence on surfaces and in positions where it could not occur.

To say that music, too, has need of scientific aid will cause still more surprise. Yet it may be shown that music is but an idealisation of the natural language of emotion; and that consequently, music must be good or bad according as it conforms to the laws of this natural language. The various inflections of voice which accompany feelings of different kinds and intensities, are the germs out of which music is developed. It is demonstrable that these inflections and cadences are not accidental or arbitrary; but that they are determined by certain general principles of vital action; and that their expressiveness depends on this. Whence it follows that musical phrases and the melodies built of them, can be effective only when they are in harmony with these general principles. It is difficult here properly to illustrate this position. But perhaps it will suffice to instance the swarms of worthless ballads that infest drawing-rooms, as compositions which science would forbid. They sin against science by setting to music ideas that are not emotional enough to prompt musical expression;

and they also sin against science by using musical phrases that have no natural relations to the ideas expressed: even where these are emotional. They are bad because they are untrue. And to say they are untrue, is to say they are unscientific.

Even in poetry the same thing holds. Like music, poetry has its root in those natural modes of expression which accompany deep feeling. Its rhythm, its strong and numerous metaphors, its hyperboles, its violent inversions, are simply exaggerations of the traits of excited speech. To be good, therefore, poetry must pay attention to those laws of nervous action which excited speech obeys. In intensifying and combining the traits of excited speech, it must have due regard to proportion—must not use its appliances without restriction; but, where the ideas are least emotional, must use the forms of poetical expression sparingly; must use them more freely as the emotion rises; and must carry them to their greatest extent, only where the emotion reaches a climax. The entire contravention of these principles results in bombast or doggerel. The insufficient respect for them is seen in didactic poetry. And it is because they are rarely fully obeyed, that so much poetry is inartistic.

Not only is it that the artist, of whatever kind, cannot produce a truthful work without he understands the laws of the phenomena he represents; but it is that he must also understand how the minds of spectators or listeners will be affected by the several peculiarities of his work—a question in psychology. What impression any art-product generates, manifestly depends upon the mental natures of those to whom it is presented; and as all mental natures have certain characteristics in common, there must result certain corresponding general principles on which alone art-products can be successfully framed. These general principles cannot be fully understood and applied, unless the artist sees how they follow from the laws of mind. To ask whether the composition of a picture is good is really to ask how the perceptions and feelings of observers will be affected by it. To ask whether a drama is well constructed, is to ask whether its situations are so arranged as duly to consult the power of attention of an audience, and duly to avoid overtaxing any one class of feelings. Equally in arranging the leading divisions of a poem or fiction, and in combining the words of a single sentence, the goodness of the effect depends upon the skill with which the mental energies and susceptibilities of the reader are economised. Every artist, in the course of his education and after-life, accumulates a stock of maxims by which his practice is regulated. Trace such maxims to their roots, and they inevitably lead you down to psychological principles. And only when the artist understands these psychological principles and their various corollaries can he work in harmony with them.

We do not for a moment believe that science will make an artist. While we contend that the leading laws both of objective and subjective phenomena must be understood by him, we by no means contend that knowledge of such laws will serve in place of natural perception. Not the poet only, but the artist of every type, is born, not made. What we assert is, that innate faculty cannot dispense with the aid of organised knowledge. Intuition will do much, but it will not do all. Only when Genius is married to Science can the highest results be produced.

As we have above asserted, Science is necessary not only for the most successful production, but also for the full appreciation, of the fine arts. In what consists the greater ability of a man than of a child to perceive the beauties of a picture; unless it is in his more extended knowledge of those truths in nature or life which the picture renders? How happens the cultivated gentleman to enjoy a fine poem so much more than a boor does; if it is not because his wider acquaintance with objects and actions enables him to see in the poem much that the boor cannot see? And if, as is here so obvious, there must be some familiarity with the things represented, before the representation can be appreciated, then, the representation can be completely appreciated only when the things represented are completely understood. The fact is, that every additional truth which a word of art expresses, gives an additional pleasure to the percipient mind—a pleasure that is missed by those ignorant of this truth. The more realities an artist indicates in any given amount of work, the more faculties does he appeal to; the more numerous ideas does he suggest; the more gratification does he afford. But to receive this gratification the spectator, listener, or reader, must know the realities which the artist has indicated; and to know these realities is to have that much science.

And now let us not overlook the further great fact, that not only does science underlie sculpture, painting, music, poetry, but that science is itself poetic. The current opinion that science and poetry are opposed, is a delusion. It is doubtless true that as states of consciousness, cognition and emotion tend to exclude each other. And it is doubtless also true that an extreme activity of the reflective powers tends to deaden the feelings; while an extreme activity of the feelings tends to deaden the reflective powers: in which sense, indeed, all orders of activity are antagonistic to each other. But it is not true that the facts of science are unpoetical; or that the cultivation of science is necessarily unfriendly to the exercise of imagination and the love of the beautiful. On the contrary, science opens up realms of poetry where to the unscientific all is a blank. Those engaged in scientific researches constantly show us that they realise not less vividly, but more vividly, than others, the poetry of their subjects. Whoso will dip into Hugh Miller's works of geology, or read Mr. Lewes's *Sea-side Studies*, will perceive that science excites poetry rather than extinguishes it. And he who contemplates the life of Goethe, must see that the poet and the man of science can co-exist in equal activity. Is it not, indeed, an absurd and almost a sacrilegious belief, that the more a man studies Nature the less he reveres it? Think you that a drop of water, which to the vulgar eye is but a drop of water, loses anything in the eye of the physicist who knows that its elements are held together by a force which, if suddenly liberated, would produce a flash of lightning? Think you that what is carelessly looked upon by the uninitiated as a mere snow-flake, does not suggest higher associations to one who had seen through a microscope the wondrously-varied and elegant forms of snow-crystals? Think you that the rounded rock marked with parallel scratches, calls up as much poetry in an ignorant mind as in the mind of a geologist, who knows that over this rock a glacier slid a million years ago? The truth is, that those who have never entered upon scientific pursuits are blind to most of the poetry by which they are surrounded. Whoever has not in youth collected plants and insects, knows not half the halo of interest which lanes and hedge-rows can assume. Whoever has not sought for fossils, has little idea of the poetical associations that surround the places where imbedded treasures were found. Whoever at the sea-side has not had a microscope and aquarium, has yet to learn what the highest pleasures of the sea-side are. Sad, indeed, is it to see how men occupy themselves with trivialities, and are indifferent to the grandest phenomena—care not to understand the architecture of the Heavens, but are deeply interested in some contemptible controversy about the intrigues of Mary Queen of Scots!—are learnedly critical over a Greek ode, and pass by without a glance that grand epic written by the finger of God upon the strata of the Earth!

We find, then, that even for this remaining division of human activities, scientific culture is the proper preparation. We find that aesthetics in general are necessarily based upon scientific principles; and can be pursued with complete success only through an acquaintance with these principles. We find that for the criticism and due appreciation of works of art, a knowledge of the constitution of things, or in other words, a knowledge of science, is requisite. And we not only find that science is the handmaid to all forms of art and poetry, but that, rightly regarded, science is itself poetic.

Thus far our question has been, the worth of knowledge of this or that kind for purposes of guidance. We have now to judge the relative value of different kinds of knowledge for purposes of discipline. This division of our subject we are obliged to treat with comparative brevity; and happily, no very lengthened treatment of it is needed. Having found what is best for the one end, we have by implication found what is best for the other. We may be quite sure that the acquirement of those classes of facts which are most useful for regulating conduct, involves a mental exercise best fitted for strengthening the faculties. It would be utterly contrary to the beautiful economy of Nature, if one kind of culture were needed for the gaining of information and another kind were needed as a mental gymnastic. Everywhere throughout creation we find faculties developed through the performance of those functions which it is their office to perform; not through the performance of artificial exercises devised to fit them for those functions. The Red Indian acquires the swiftness and agility which make him a successful hunter, by the actual pursuit of animals; and through the miscellaneous activities of his life, he gains a better balance of physical powers than gymnastics ever give. That skill in tracking enemies and prey which he had reached after long practice, implies a subtlety of perception far exceeding anything produced by artificial training. And similarly in all cases. From the Bushman whose eye, habitually employed in identifying distant objects that are to be pursued or fled from, has acquired a telescopic range, to the accountant whose daily practice enables him to add up several columns of figures simultaneously; we find that the highest power of a faculty results from the discharge of those duties which the conditions of life require it to discharge. And we may be certain, *à priori*, that the same law holds throughout education. The education of most value for guidance, must at the same time be the education of most value for discipline. Let us consider the evidence.

One advantage claimed for that devotion to language-learning which forms so prominent a feature in the ordinary *curriculum*, is, that the memory is thereby strengthened. This is assumed to be an advantage peculiar to the study of words. But the truth is, that the sciences afford far wider fields for the exercise of memory. It is no slight task to remember everything about our solar system; much more to remember all that is known concerning the structure of our galaxy. The number of compound substances, to which chemistry daily adds, is so great that few, save professors, can enumerate them; and to recollect the atomic constitutions and affinities of all these compounds, is scarcely possible without making chemistry the occupation of life. In the enormous mass of phenomena presented by the Earth's crust, and in the still more enormous mass of phenomena presented by the fossils it contains, there is matter which it takes the geological student years of application to master. Each leading division of physics—sound, heat, light, electricity—includes facts numerous enough to alarm any one proposing to learn them all. And when we pass to the organic sciences, the effort of memory required becomes still greater. In human anatomy alone, the quantity of detail is so great, that the young surgeon has commonly to get it up half-a-dozen times before he can permanently retain it. The number of species of plants which botanists distinguish, amounts to some 320,000; while the varied forms of animal life with which the zoologist deals, are estimated at some 2,000,000. So vast is the accumulation of facts which men of science have before them, that only by dividing and subdividing their labours can they deal with it. To a detailed knowledge of his own division, each adds but a general knowledge of the allied ones; joined perhaps to a rudimentary acquaintance with some others. Surely, then, science, cultivated even to a very moderate extent, affords adequate exercise for memory. To say the very least, it involves quite as good a discipline for this faculty as language does.

But now mark that while, for the training of mere memory, science is as good as, if not better than, language; it has an immense superiority in the kind of memory it trains. In the acquirement of a language, the connections of ideas to be established in the mind correspond to facts that are in great measure accidental; whereas, in the acquirement of science, the connections of ideas to be established in the mind correspond to facts that are mostly necessary. It is true that the relations of words to their meanings are in one sense natural; that the genesis of these relations may be traced back a certain distance, though rarely to the beginning; and that the laws of this genesis form a branch of mental science—the science of philology. But since it will not be contended that in the acquisition of languages, as ordinarily carried on, these natural relations between words and their meanings are habitually traced, and their laws explained; it must be admitted that they are commonly learned as fortuitous relations. On the other hand, the relations which science presents are causal relations; and, when properly taught, are understood as such. While language familiarises with non-rational relations, science familiarises with rational relations. While the one exercises memory only, the other exercises both memory and understanding.

Observe next, that a great superiority of science over language as a means of discipline, is, that it cultivates the judgment. As, in a lecture on mental education delivered at the Royal Institution, Professor Faraday well remarks, the most common intellectual fault is deficiency of judgment. "Society, speaking generally," he says, "is not only ignorant as respects education of the judgment, but it is also ignorant of its ignorance." And the cause to which he ascribes this state, is want of scientific culture. The truth of his conclusion is obvious. Correct judgment with regard to surrounding objects, events, and consequences, becomes possible only through knowledge of the way in which surrounding phenomena depend on each other. No extent of acquaintance with the meanings of words, will guarantee correct inferences respecting causes and effects. The habit of drawing conclusions from data, and then of verifying those conclusions by observation and experiment, can alone give the power of judging correctly. And that it necessitates this habit is one of the immense advantages of science.

Not only, however, for intellectual discipline is science the best; but also for *moral* discipline. The learning of languages tends, if anything, further to increase the already undue respect for authority. Such and such are the meanings of these words, says the teacher of the dictionary. So and so is the rule in this case, says the grammar. By the pupil these dicta are received as unquestionable. His constant attitude of mind is that of submission to dogmatic teaching. And a necessary result is a tendency to accept without inquiry whatever is established. Quite opposite is the mental tone generated by the cultivation of science. Science makes constant appeal to individual reason. Its truths are not accepted on authority alone; but all are at liberty to test them—nay, in many cases, the pupil is required to think out his own conclusions. Every step in a scientific investigation is submitted to his judgment. He is not asked to admit it without seeing it to be true. And the trust in his own powers thus produced is further increased by the uniformity with which Nature justifies his inferences when they are correctly drawn. From all which there flows that independence which is a most valuable element in character. Nor is this the only moral benefit bequeathed by scientific culture. When carried on, as it should always be, as much as possible under the form of original research, it exercises perseverance and sincerity. As says Professor Tyndall of inductive inquiry, "It requires patient industry, and an humble and conscientious acceptance of what Nature reveals. The first condition of success is an honest receptivity and a willingness to abandon all preconceived notions, however cherished, if they be found to contradict the truth. Believe me, a self-renunciation which has something noble in it, and of which the world never hears, is often enacted in the private experience of the true votary of science."

Lastly we have to assert—and the assertion will, we doubt not, cause extreme surprise—that the discipline of science is superior to that of our ordinary education, because of the *religious* culture that it gives. Of course we do not here use the words scientific and religious in their ordinary limited acceptations; but in their widest and highest acceptations. Doubtless, to the superstitions that pass under the name of religion, science is antagonistic; but not to the essential religion which these superstitions merely hide. Doubtless, too, in much of the science that is current, there is a pervading spirit of irreligion; but not in that true science which had passed beyond the superficial into the profound.

"True science and true religion," says Professor Huxley at the close of a recent course of lectures, "are twin-sisters, and the separation of either from the other is sure to prove the death of both. Science prospers exactly in proportion as it is religious; and religion flourishes in exact proportion to the scientific depth and firmness of its basis. The great deeds of philosophers have been less the fruit of their intellect than of the direction of that intellect by an eminently religious tone of mind. Truth has yielded herself rather to their patience, their love, their single-heartedness, and their self-denial, than to their logical acumen."

So far from science being irreligious, as many think, it is the neglect of science that is irreligious—it is the refusal to study the surrounding creation that is irreligious. Take a humble simile. Suppose a writer were daily saluted with praises couched in superlative language. Suppose the wisdom, the grandeur, the beauty of his works, were the constant topics of the eulogies addressed to him. Suppose those who unceasingly uttered these eulogies on his works were content with looking at the outsides of them; and had never opened them, much less tried to understand them. What value should we put upon their praises? What should we think of their sincerity? Yet, comparing small things to great, such is the conduct of mankind in general, in reference to the Universe and its Cause. Nay, it is worse. Not only do they pass by without study, these things which they daily proclaim to be so wonderful; but very frequently they condemn as mere triflers those who give time to the observation of Nature—they actually scorn those who show any active interest in these marvels. We repeat, then, that not science, but the neglect of science, is irreligious. Devotion to science, is a tacit worship—a tacit recognition of worth in the things studied; and by implication in their Cause. It is not a mere lip-homage, but a homage expressed in actions—not a mere professed respect, but a respect proved by the sacrifice of time, thought, and labour.

Nor is it thus only that true science is essentially religious. It is religious, too, inasmuch as it generates a profound respect for, and an implicit faith in, those uniformities of action which all things disclose. By accumulated experiences the man of science acquires a thorough belief in the unchanging relations of phenomena—in the invariable connection of cause and consequence—in the necessity of good or evil results. Instead of the rewards and punishments of traditional belief, which people vaguely hope they may gain, or escape, spite of their disobedience; he finds that there are rewards and punishments in the ordained constitution of things; and that the evil results of disobedience are inevitable. He sees that the laws to which we must submit are both inexorable and beneficent. He sees that in conforming to them, the process of things is ever towards a greater perfection and a higher happiness.

Hence he is led constantly to insist on them, and is indignant when they are disregarded. And thus does he, by asserting the eternal principles of things and the necessity of obeying them, prove himself intrinsically religious.

Add lastly the further religious aspect of science, that it alone can give us true conceptions of ourselves and our relation to the mysteries of existence. At the same time that it shows us all which can be known, it shows us the limits beyond which we can know nothing. Not by dogmatic assertion, does it teach the impossibility of comprehending the Ultimate Cause of things; but it leads us clearly to recognise this impossibility by bringing us in every direction to boundaries we cannot cross. It realises to us in a way which nothing else can, the littleness of human intelligence in the face of that which transcends human intelligence. While towards the traditions and authorities of men its attitude may be proud, before the impenetrable veil which hides the Absolute its attitude is humble—a true pride and a true humility. Only the sincere man of science and by this title we do not mean the mere calculator of distances, or analyser of compounds, or labeller of species; but him who through lower truths seeks higher, and eventually the highest—only the genuine man of science, we say, can truly know how utterly beyond, not only human knowledge but human conception, is the Universal Power of which Nature, and Life, and Thought are manifestations.

We conclude, then, that for discipline, as well as for guidance, science is of chiefest value. In all its effects, learning the meanings of things, is better than learning the meanings of words. Whether for intellectual, moral, or religious training, the study of surrounding phenomena is immensely superior to the study of grammars and lexicons.

Thus to the question we set out with—What knowledge is of most worth?—the uniform reply is—Science. This is the verdict on all the counts. For direct self-preservation, or the maintenance of life and health, the all-important knowledge is—Science. For that indirect self-preservation which we call gaining a livelihood, the knowledge of greatest value is—Science. For the due discharge of parental functions, the proper guidance is to be found only in—Science. For that interpretation of national life, past and present, without which the citizen cannot rightly regulate his conduct, the indispensable key is—Science. Alike for the most perfect production and highest enjoyment of art in all its forms, the needful preparation is still—Science. And for purposes of discipline—intellectual, moral, religious—the most efficient study is, once more—Science. The question which at first seemed so perplexed, has become, in the course of our inquiry, comparatively simple. We have not to estimate the degrees of importance of different orders of human activity, and different studies as severally fitting us for them; since we find that the study of Science, in its most comprehensive meaning, is the best preparation for all these orders of activity. We have not to decide between the claims of knowledge of great though conventional value, and knowledge of less though intrinsic value; seeing that the knowledge which proves to be of most value in all other respects, is intrinsically most valuable: its worth is not dependent upon opinion, but is as fixed as is the relation of man to the surrounding world. Necessary and eternal as are its truths, all Science concerns all mankind for all time. Equally at present and in the remotest future, must it be of incalculable importance for the regulation of their conduct, that men should understand the science of life, physical, mental, and social; and that they should understand all other science as a key to the science of life.

And yet this study, immensely transcending all other in importance, is that which, in an age of boasted education, receives the least attention. While what we call civilisation could never have arisen had it not been for science, science forms scarcely an appreciable element in our so-called civilised training. Though to the progress of science we owe it, that millions find support where once there was food only for thousands; yet of these millions but a few thousands pay any respect to that which has made their existence possible. Though increasing knowledge of the properties and relations of things has not only enabled wandering tribes to grow into populous nations, but has given to the countless members of these populous nations, comforts and pleasures which their few naked ancestors never even conceived, or could have believed, yet is this kind of knowledge only now receiving a grudging recognition in our highest educational institutions. To the slowly growing acquaintance with the uniform co-existences and sequences of phenomena—to the establishment of invariable laws, we owe our emancipation from the grossest superstitions. But for science we should be still worshipping fetishes; or, with hecatombs of victims, propitiating diabolical deities. And yet this science, which, in place of the most degrading conceptions of things, has given us some insight into the grandeurs of creation, is written against in our theologies and frowned upon from our pulpits.

Paraphrasing an Eastern fable, we may say that in the family of knowledges, Science is the household drudge, who, in obscurity, hides unrecognised perfections. To her has been committed all the works; by her skill, intelligence, and devotion, have all conveniences and gratifications been obtained; and while ceaselessly ministering to the rest, she has been kept in the background, that her haughty sisters might flaunt their fripperies in the eyes of the world. The parallel holds yet further. For we are fast coming to the *dénouement*, when the positions will be changed; and while these haughty sisters sink into merited neglect, Science, proclaimed as highest alike in worth and beauty, will reign supreme.

INTELLECTUAL EDUCATION

There cannot fail to be a relationship between the successive systems of education, and the successive social states with which they have co-existed. Having a common origin in the national mind, the institutions of each epoch, whatever be their special functions, must have a family likeness. When men received their creed and its interpretations from an infallible authority deigning no explanations, it was natural that the teaching of children should be purely dogmatic. While "believe and ask no questions" was the maxim of the Church, it was fitly the maxim of the school. Conversely, now that Protestantism has gained for adults a right of private judgment and established the practice of appealing to reason, there is harmony in the change that has made juvenile instruction a process of exposition addressed to the understanding. Along with political despotism, stern in its commands, ruling by force of terror, visiting trifling crimes with death, and implacable in its vengeance on the disloyal, there necessarily grew up an academic discipline similarly harsh—a discipline of multiplied injunctions and blows for every breach of them—a discipline of unlimited autocracy upheld by rods, and ferules, and the black-hole. On the other hand, the increase of political liberty, the abolition of laws restricting individual action, and the amelioration of the criminal code, have been accompanied by a kindred progress towards non-coercive education: the pupil is hampered by fewer restraints, and other means than punishments are used to govern him. In those ascetic days when men, acting on the greatest-misery principle, held that the more gratifications they denied themselves the more virtuous they were, they, as a matter of course, considered that the best education which most thwarted the wishes of their children, and cut short all spontaneous activity with—"You mustn't do so." While, on the contrary, now that happiness is coming to be regarded as a legitimate aim—now that hours of labour are being shortened and popular recreations provided—parents and teachers are beginning to see that most childish desires may rightly be gratified, that childish sports should be encouraged, and that the tendencies of the growing mind are not altogether so diabolical as was supposed. The age in which all believed that trades must be established by bounties and prohibitions; that manufacturers needed their materials and qualities and prices to be prescribed; and that the value of money could be determined by law; was an age which unavoidably cherished the notions that a child's mind could be made to order; that its powers were to be imparted by the schoolmaster; that it was a receptacle into which knowledge was to be put, and there built up after the teacher's ideal. In this free-trade era, however, when we are learning that there is much more self-regulation in things than was supposed; that labour, and commerce, and agriculture, and navigation, can do better without management than with it; that political governments, to be efficient, must grow up from within and not be imposed from without; we are also being taught that there is a natural process of mental evolution which is not to be disturbed without injury; that we may not force on the unfolding mind our artificial forms; but that psychology, also, discloses to us a law of supply and demand to which, if we would not do harm, we must conform. Thus, alike in its oracular dogmatism, in its harsh discipline, in its multiplied restrictions, in its professed asceticism, and in its faith in the devices of men, the old educational regime was akin to the social systems with which it was contemporaneous; and similarly, in the reverse of these characteristics, our modern modes of culture correspond to our more liberal religious and political institutions.

But there remain further parallelisms to which we have not yet adverted: that, namely, between the processes by which these respective changes have been wrought out; and that between the several states of heterogeneous opinion to which they have led. Some centuries ago there was uniformity of belief—religious, political, and educational. All men were Romanists, all were Monarchists, all were disciples of Aristotle; and no one thought of calling in question that grammar-school routine under which all were brought up. The same agency has in each case replaced this uniformity by a constantly-increasing diversity. That tendency towards assertion of the individuality, which, after contributing to produce the great Protestant movement, has since gone on to produce an ever-increasing number of sects—that tendency which initiated political parties, and out of the two primary ones has, in these modern days, evolved a multiplicity to which every year adds—that tendency which led to the Baconian rebellion against the schools, and has since originated here and abroad, sundry new systems of thought—is a tendency which, in education also, has caused divisions and the accumulation of methods. As external consequences of the same internal change, these processes have necessarily been more or less simultaneous. The decline of authority, whether papal, philosophic, kingly, or tutorial, is essentially one phenomenon; in each of its aspects a leaning towards free action is seen alike in the working out of the change itself, and in the new forms of theory and practice to which the change has given birth.

While many will regret this multiplication of schemes of juvenile culture, the catholic observer will discern in it a means of ensuring the final establishment of a rational system. Whatever may be thought of theological dissent, it is clear that dissent in education results in facilitating inquiry by the division in labour. Were we in possession of the true method, divergence from it would, of course, be prejudicial; but the true method having to be found, the efforts of numerous independent seekers carrying out their researches in different directions, constitute a better agency for finding it than any that could be devised. Each of them struck by some new thought which probably contains more or less of basis in facts— each of them zealous on behalf of his plan, fertile in expedients to test its correctness, and untiring in his efforts to make known its success—each of them merciless in his criticism on the rest; there cannot fail, by composition of forces, to be a gradual approximation of all towards the right course. Whatever portion of the normal method any one has discovered, must, by the constant exhibition of its results, force itself into adoption; whatever wrong practices he has joined with it must, by repeated experiment and failure, be exploded. And by this aggregation of truths and elimination of errors, there must eventually be developed a correct and complete body of doctrine. Of the three phases through which human opinion passes—the unanimity of the ignorant, the disagreement of the inquiring, and the unanimity of the wise—it is manifest that the second is the parent of the third. They are not sequences in time only, they are sequences in causation. However impatiently, therefore, we may witness the present conflict of educational systems, and however much we may regret its accompanying evils, we must recognise it as a transition stage needful to be passed through, and beneficent in its ultimate effects.

Meanwhile, may we not advantageously take stock of our progress? After fifty years of discussion, experiment, and comparison of results, may we not expect a few steps towards the goal to be already made good? Some old methods must by this time have fallen out of use; some new ones must have become established; and many others must be in process of general abandonment or adoption. Probably we may see in these various changes, when put side by side, similar characteristics—may find in them a common tendency; and so, by inference, may get a clue to the direction in which experience is leading us, and gather hints how we may achieve yet further improvements. Let us then, as a preliminary to a deeper consideration of the matter, glance at the leading contrasts between the education of the past and that of the present.

The suppression of every error is commonly followed by a temporary ascendency of the contrary one; and so it happened, that after the ages when physical development alone was aimed at, there came an age when culture of the mind was the sole solicitude—when children had lesson-books put before them at between two and three years old, and the getting of knowledge was thought the one thing needful. As, further, it usually happens that after one of these reactions the next advance is achieved by co-ordinating the antagonist errors, and perceiving that they are opposite sides of one truth; so, we are now coming to the conviction that body and mind must both be cared for, and the whole thing being unfolded. The forcing-system has been, by many, given up; and precocity is discouraged. People are beginning to see that the first requisite to success in life, is to be a good animal. The best brain is found of little service, if there be not enough vital energy to work it; and hence to obtain the one by sacrificing the source of the other, is now considered a folly—a folly which the eventual failure of juvenile prodigies constantly illustrates. Thus we are discovering the wisdom of the saying, that one secret in education is "to know how wisely to lose time."

The once universal practice of learning by rote, is daily falling more into discredit. All modern authorities condemn the old mechanical way of teaching the alphabet. The multiplication table is now frequently taught experimentally. In the acquirement of languages, the grammar-school plan is being superseded by plans based on the spontaneous process followed by the child in gaining its mother tongue. Describing the methods there used, the "Reports on the Training School at Battersea" say:—"The instruction in the whole preparatory course is chiefly oral, and is illustrated as much as possible by appeals to nature." And so throughout. The rote-system, like ether systems of its age, made more of the forms and symbols than of the things symbolised. To repeat the words correctly was everything; to understand their meaning nothing; and thus the spirit was sacrificed to the letter. It is at length perceived that, in this case as in others, such a result is not accidental but necessary—that in proportion as there is attention to the signs, there must be inattention to the things signified; or that, as Montaigne long ago said—*Sçavoir par cœur n'est pas sçavoir.*

Along with rote-teaching, is declining also the nearly-allied teaching by rules. The particulars first, and then the generalisation, is the new method—a method, as the Battersea School Reports remarks, which, though "the reverse of the method usually followed, which consists in giving the pupil the rule first," is yet proved by experience to be the right one. Rule-teaching is now condemned as imparting a merely empirical knowledge—as producing an appearance of understanding without the reality. To give the net product of inquiry, without the inquiry that leads to it, is found to be both enervating and inefficient. General truths to be of due and permanent use, must be earned. "Easy come easy go," is a saying as applicable to knowledge as to wealth. While rules, lying isolated in the mind—not joined to its other contents as out-growths from them—are continually forgotten; the principles which those rules express piecemeal, become, when once reached by the understanding, enduring possessions. While the rule-taught youth is at sea when beyond his rules, the youth instructed in principles solves a new case as readily as an old one. Between a mind of rules and a mind of principles, there exists a difference such as that between a confused heap of materials, and the same materials organised into a complete whole, with all its parts bound together. Of which types this last has not only the advantage that its constituent parts are better retained, but the much greater advantage that it forms an efficient agent for inquiry, for independent thought, for discovery—ends for which the first is useless. Nor let it be supposed that this is a simile only: it is the literal truth. The union of facts into generalisations *is* the organisation of knowledge, whether considered as an objective phenomenon or a subjective one; and the mental grasp may be measured by the extent to which this organisation is carried.

From the substitution of principles for rules, and the necessarily co-ordinate practice of leaving abstractions untaught till the mind has been familiarised with the facts from which they are abstracted, has resulted the postponement of some once early studies to a late period. This is exemplified in the abandonment of that intensely stupid custom, the teaching of grammar to children. As M. Marcel says:—"It may without hesitation be affirmed that grammar is not the stepping-stone, but the finishing instrument." As Mr. Wyse argues:—"Grammar and Syntax are a collection of laws and rules. Rules are gathered from practice; they are the results of induction to which we come by long observation and comparison of facts. It is, in fine, the science, the philosophy of language. In following the process of nature, neither individuals nor nations ever arrive at the science *first*. A language is spoken, and poetry written, many years before either a grammar or prosody is even thought of. Men did not wait till Aristotle had constructed his logic, to reason." In short, as grammar was made after language, so ought it to be taught after language: an inference which all who recognise the relationship between the evolution of the race and that of the individual, will see to be unavoidable.

Of new practices that have grown up during the decline of these old ones, the most important is the systematic culture of the powers of observation. After long ages of blindness, men are at last seeing that the spontaneous activity of the observing faculties in children has a meaning and a use. What was once thought mere purposeless action, or play, or mischief, as the case might be, is now recognised as the process of acquiring a knowledge on which all after-knowledge is based. Hence the well-conceived but ill-conducted system of *object-*

lessons. The saying of Bacon, that physics is the mother of the sciences, has come to have a meaning in education. Without an accurate acquaintance with the visible and tangible properties of things, our conceptions must be erroneous, our inferences fallacious, and our operations unsuccessful. "The education of the senses neglected, all after education partakes of a drowsiness, a haziness, an insufficiency, which it is impossible to cure." Indeed, if we consider it, we shall find that exhaustive observation is an element in all great success. It is not to artists, naturalists, and men of science only, that it is needful; it is not only that the physician depends on it for the correctness of his diagnosis, and that to the engineer it is so important that some years in the workshop are prescribed for him; but we may see that the philosopher, also, is fundamentally one who *observes* relationships of things which others had overlooked, and that the poet, too, is one who *sees* the fine facts in nature which all recognise when pointed out, but did not before remark. Nothing requires more to be insisted on than that vivid and complete impressions are all-essential. No sound fabric of wisdom can be woven out of a rotten raw-material.

While the old method of presenting truths in the abstract has been falling out of use, there has been a corresponding adoption of the new method of presenting them in the concrete. The rudimentary facts of exact science are now being learnt by direct intuition, as textures, and tastes, and colours are learnt. Employing the ball-frame for first lessons in arithmetic exemplifies this. It is well illustrated, too, in Professor De Morgan's mode of explaining the decimal notation. M. Marcel, rightly repudiating the old system of tables, teaches weights and measures by referring to the actual yard and foot, pound and ounce, gallon and quart; and lets the discovery of their relationships be experimental. The use of geographical models and models of the regular bodies, etc., as introductory to geography and geometry respectively, are facts of the same class. Manifestly, a common trait of these methods is, that they carry each child's mind through a process like that which the mind of humanity at large has gone through. The truths of number, of form, of relationship in position, were all originally drawn from objects; and to present these truths to the child in the concrete is to let him learn them as the race learnt them. By and by, perhaps, it will be seen that he cannot possibly learn them in any other way; for that if he is made to repeat them as abstractions, the abstractions can have no meaning for him, until he finds that they are simply statements of what he intuitively discerns.

But of all the changes taking place, the most significant is the growing desire to make the acquirement of knowledge pleasurable rather than painful—a desire based on the more or less distinct perception, that at each age the intellectual action which a child likes is a healthful one for it; and conversely. There is a spreading opinion that the rise of an appetite for any kind of information implies that the unfolding mind has become fit to assimilate it, and needs it for purposes of growth; and that, on the other hand, the disgust felt towards such information is a sign either that it is prematurely presented, or that it is presented in an indigestible form. Hence the efforts to make early education amusing, and all education interesting. Hence the lectures on the value of play. Hence the defence of nursery rhymes and fairy tales. Daily we more and more conform our plans to juvenile opinion. Does the child like this or that kind of teaching?—does he take to it? we constantly ask. "His natural desire of variety should be indulged," says M. Marcel; "and the gratification of his curiosity should be combined with his improvement." "Lessons," he again remarks, "should cease before the child evinces symptoms of weariness." And so with later education. Short breaks during school-hours, excursions into the country, amusing lectures, choral songs—in these and many like traits the change may be discerned. Asceticism is disappearing out of education as out of life; and the usual test of political legislation—its tendency to promote happiness—is beginning to be, in a great degree, the test of legislation for the school and the nursery.

What now is the common characteristic of these several changes? Is it not an increasing conformity to the methods of Nature? The relinquishment of early forcing, against which Nature rebels, and the leaving of the first years for exercise of the limbs and senses, show this. The superseding of rote-learnt lessons by lessons orally and experimentally given, like those of the field and play-ground, shows this. The disuse of rule-teaching, and the adoption of teaching by principles—that is, the leaving of generalisations until there are particulars to base them on—show this. The system of object-lessons shows this. The teaching of the rudiments of science in the concrete instead of the abstract, shows this. And above all, this tendency is shown in the variously-directed efforts to present knowledge in attractive forms, and so to make the acquirement of it pleasurable. For, as it is the order of Nature in all creatures that the gratification accompanying the fulfilment of needful functions serves as a stimulus to their fulfilment—as, during the self-education of the young child, the delight taken in the biting of corals and the pulling to pieces of toys, becomes the prompter to actions which teach it the properties of matter; it follows that, in choosing the succession of subjects and the modes of instruction which most interest the pupil, we are fulfilling Nature's behests, and adjusting our proceedings to the laws of life.

www.ingramcontent.com/pod-product-compliance
Lightning Source LLC
Chambersburg PA
CBHW080023130526
44591CB00036B/2633